Candace Mezetin has an immense love and passion for writing. It is the truest window to her soul. Since the age of eight, she has been writing short stories and poetry. Candace has worked as an occupational therapist for seven years, after which she home-schooled her four children for five years. She currently teaches science and math and is also a certified fitness instructor, but writing is her first love. Candace is a devoted mother to her four children, and has purposed her life towards leaving a legacy for them that will forever shine bright.

To all the women who have ever felt helpless, hopeless and voiceless, this book is for you. I pray that this story will help you to find your voice and that it gives you the courage to stand up and proclaim your truth, unapologetically.

Candace Mezetin

BIRTHED ANEW: FROM PAIN TO PASSION TO PURPOSE

AUSTIN MACAULEY PUBLISHERS™

LONDON • CAMBRIDGE • NEW YORK • SHARJAH

Ordering Information
Quantity sales: Special discounts are available on quantity purchases by corporations, associations, and others. For details, contact the publisher at the address below.

Publisher's Cataloging-in-Publication data
Mezetin, Candace
Birthed Anew: From Pain to Passion to Purpose

ISBN 9798886935271 (Paperback)
ISBN 9798886935288 (ePub e-book)

Library of Congress Control Number: 2023920488

www.austinmacauley.com/us

First Published 2024
Austin Macauley Publishers LLC
40 Wall Street, 33rd Floor, Suite 3302
New York, NY 10005
USA

mail-usa@austinmacauley.com
+1 (646) 5125767

God.

I thank you God for giving me the opportunity to pour my heart out on paper, to translate moaning into words, and tears into joy. Writing this story has transformed my life, and I am honoured that such a mess of a story could be turned into a powerful message to empower others.

I would like to thank Brandon Knopp for being a conduit where which I could express the traumatic incidences in my life. He has been a source of encouragement and guide during the formation of this book.

I want to express my utmost gratitude to everyone who has walked with me along this journey. To those who have lifted me up when I was weak, and who prayed with me and for me, thank you. I love you all.

Foreword by Shadé – Holistic Health Mentor

There's a difference between passion and purpose.

You can be passionate about some things and still not be walking in your purpose.

But if you are walking in your purpose, you will most certainly always be passionate.

Passion is the vehicle that guides you to purpose. It's the north star if you will for approaching big revelation for your life.

Sometimes revelation comes like an unexpected lightning bolt that takes you by surprise lighting up the whole night sky giving you the biggest aha moment ever.

Other times revelation comes in pieces like a 1,000 piece puzzle that you assemble bit by bit as you go along.

But what do you do with those puzzle pieces or that big aha moment?

When you're able to see the vision, understand your purpose, but don't see 'the how' it can feel overwhelming. You may feel blindsided or paralyzed by fear because you lack certain gifts to walk out the vision effectively.

That's when faith has to be activated.

When you walk in your purpose God will confirm time and time again that you are exactly where you need to be.

As you yield to Him, He will send help to fill in the gaps here and there. He will send strangers who become like family. He will send impartation of directions that come as a whisper, or felt like a light tap on the shoulder.

It may not be understood by others,
But that's not any of your concern.
Your end all goal is walking in obedience to build, and pursue something so much bigger than you.

Remember…
God doesn't call the qualified.
He qualifies the called.

He's called you child of God. Have you answered?
Everything is in place. It's time to walk with childlike faith.
Passion is pulling and purpose is awaiting.

Abundant blessings.

Table of Contents

By Candace Therese Mezetin

Brokenness was for yesterday. Today has finally come. I live healed. Healed from the silence that barricaded me from experiencing the fullness that life has to offer. Healed from the mental groanings that were resurrected from the core of my soul, never escaping, but marinating in my mind...over and over and over again. Brokenness was yesterday's tune, but today, I sing a new song.

This is a story of how abandonment, betrayal, and eventually courage can foster the birth of a renewed soul and mind through the passageway of forgiveness. Birthed Anew is the portrayed revelation of one's authentic journey through self-identification, self-reflection, self-expression, self-discovery, self-renewal, and lastly the pinnacle of self-love which is the key ingredient to the development of a whole person. The bitterness of life can afford the opportunity to seek growth and betterment as we aim to maximize our truest and fullest potential as essential contributors to society.

Prologue

My heart was now racing a million miles an hour. The knot in my stomach regurgitated into my throat and breathing became a chore. I was unsure of what was about to happen, even though I was smart enough to figure it out. Instinctually, the door was the goal. If I could find a way to hoist him off me, maybe I could escape. I couldn't get my legs to move. The strength I envisioned in my mind did not translate to my body. Execution failed…

"Mommy, help me…" were the only words I managed to whisper.

Tears gushed down my face like a streaming wild river. I wanted to live and fought to stay present with every gasp of air. Each breath was short and swift.

I cried.

I died.

I lost myself and I had no power.

I lay helpless, with the streams of tears continuing to flow. My chest was saturated with a compilation of sweat and tears. How did I end up here? Oh yes, it was all my fault. I should never have asked him to help me.

Instantly, I fell backward into a sea of blackness. The only sounds heard were my piercing cries. My heart was lodged in my throat, arms waving aimlessly as I fell. Falling faster and faster and faster…until I hit rock bottom and died.

Numbness equates to death. The dead person cannot feel anything. The dead person has no thoughts, nor can they display any emotions. There I was dead. Living a numb life is detrimental to one's being. You don't know what you know and you're completely oblivious to what you don't know. You pretty much just exist, and that is all. No good thing can yield from a numb soul.

I tell myself that I must wake up from this life of numbness. Taking a moment to explore and assess the environment can be a key to unlocking this dreaded door. I look around with intensity and intentionality. The world is in front of me, beautifully arranged. The glorious mountains are enshrouded by floral arrangements of red, yellow, green, and orange as fall creates her space for temporary lodgment. Birds glide freely across the vast, blue sky and the sun bashfully hides behind the clouds playing peek-a-boo with me. I wish I were in the mood to play along.

I know I have been hiding lately. It's dark where I live, and this is how I like it. I wander here daily and as I peruse my space; I feel the sharp rocks creating grooves underneath my bare feet. The quiet drops of water slide down the cool, clammy walls, and I rest my head against its rocky surface. I close my eyes. Life exists all around me, but I'm absent to the present eyes. I'm screaming for help, but the world persists in its current state, without one reacting to my cries.

I close my book.

"This is so hard for me to write!"

I cry out into the cusp of the night. My voice echoes into the darkness and is carried away into complete silence. I sat there in anticipation of a response. Someone who would give me a word of hope, and encouragement. I needed to get this assignment done. There was so much to say, and I didn't know how much or how little to reveal. Do I start from the very beginning? Or do I just focus on my present issues? Is there a way that my past issues connect with my present issues? I needed guidance! A compass maybe, to steer me in the right direction.

I placed my book in my backpack and dragged my feet into the house to hit the hay.

Chapter 1: Today

"Alright, class! Settle down!" shouted Professor De Jesus as he feverishly waved his hands to capture our attention.

He spent about three minutes in auditory combat as he sought to regain control of a boisterous classroom. Professor De Jesus stood about five feet tall with a wide stance. He was a Caucasian male with a small stature but a big personality. His flamboyant ways always found a way to seep through, and even though the class tended to take a moment to settle down, we loved him, and eventually calmed down.

"Welcome to week eight of Explorations of the Mind."

The class erupted in a loud, booming, explosive roar as we were nearing the end of the course. I had taken it upon myself to enroll in some enrichment courses as part of my quest to improve myself. Obviously, I had some real problems that needed to be addressed. Here I sit in a classroom filled with young adults, fresh out of high school! It was certainly in my favor that I did not look a day older than 25. I mixed well with the crowd on a physical level, but they were no match for me on any other level.

To be honest, I enjoyed this class. It was a class that sought to identify how the mind and various thought patterns were connected to behaviors. This course sought to explore how one's mindset could be manipulated to affect a change in behaviors. This course is exactly what I needed.

"For the last eight weeks, we have been exploring different aspects of 'the self' and two weeks ago, I assigned you all the final project entitled, 'Who Am I?' How many of you already began formulating your ideas on what you will present?"

I looked around to see how many hands were raised, and to no avail, not one single hand went up, including my own.

"Oh boy, there is not that much time remaining before we have to present so I implore you all, to get on with your assignment. I want to remind you that this assignment is giving us the framework to explore how our experiences mold and shape us. In essence, how our experiences develop us into who we become, and how we relate to the world around us. We will continue to assess who we are and determine whether we are at a place of peace and acceptance or if there are areas in our lives that we need to improve in order to live out our truest purpose and calling," explained Professor De Jesus.

I swallowed hard, and I tried not to focus on the beads of sweat that forced their way out of my pores. I wonder if anyone noticed. If I didn't pay any attention to it, no one else would. My eyes became glossy, and everyone seemed to be dancing and swaying from side to side.

Feelings from the other night swarmed over me as I recalled my frustration on the back deck. There were so many things that I could explore that were significant in the development of 'myself', but what do I include? My mind drifted down memory lane. I fell into a reminiscent state of old experiences that flooded the forefront of my mind.

Professor De Jesus's voice grew muffled and between the sweat and silent tears, my eyes burned. My classmates appeared as pieces of moving abstract art, and Professor De Jesus was the biggest blob. My heart began to beat in a syncopated rhythm that was rowdy in my ears. The drum assimilation became unbearable. The thought of facing myself was so overwhelming at times. Fear swept over me, and I became paralyzed. I sat and stared at Professor De Jesus in a catatonic state.

Chapter 2: Yesterday

Before my existence, there was Daddy and Mommy. The two beings from which my genetic makeup is derived. Everything about me came from them. They lived on the beautiful Island of Jamaica; a small paradise strategically placed in the Caribbean Sea. The place where palm trees swayed in the wind and the water beamed with bright colors of crystal blue. The beautiful array of fish could be seen swimming for miles and miles on end. Jamaica, the place where you could watch the sun lay to rest over her ocean bed.

As a young girl, I had life 'made' and life was good! I resided in a beautiful ranch house located in the heart of the 'hood', Jamaica Queens, NY. The rancid smell of urine permeated the streets, and empty containers of all sorts 'decorated' the sidewalks from corner to corner. Gun shots could be heard piercing through the crisp of the night on a nightly basis. It wasn't the best place for children to be raised. But, even amidst the overbearing qualities of my neighborhood, my house was a rose amongst a bunch of thorns. My house had a veranda that portrayed a solid red and white hue which for me signified love and purity. There was a huge yard that encircled the house with enough space to run, play and be free, just as a child should be.

I had my own room with my own T.V., a small one that is, but you better believe I was a happy little girl. I remember those late nights when I should have been sleeping, but instead, I was awake watching late-night episodes of 'Cheers'. The room was dark and the light from the T.V. illuminated the room. That memory brings a warm smile to my very core.

I remember those warm summer days when swimming in the little plastic pool that Daddy bought for me, and my siblings were our wont. The pool scratched our skin every time we jumped in, but that did not prevent us from enjoying its amenities. It had a mini slide that swirled around and ended in the 'bigger' part of the little pool. Jumping in and waddling out was my thing. I remember lying down in that pool pretending that I was a great fish in the ocean, flapping my fins vigorously, still yet not moving anywhere. I remember my little two-piece bathing suit with my little, big belly sticking out. Truth be told, I was a plump little girl. Round with short, picky hair. I had hair that made Brillo pads seem soft.

I remember the playground set that we had in the backyard. It had two swings, a slide, and a seesaw that my sister and I rode together quite often. Up and down, up and down we would go. It was an activity that we engaged in for hours upon hours, only stopping to the scream of our mother calling us in for either lunch or dinner. Our backyard was filled with grass, rich and green. It was a backyard where vegetables and fruits grew along the perimeter.

Tomatoes, strawberries, cucumbers, and peppers were regular foods on our plates, and they were truly the best-tasting fruits and vegetables I remember.

I remember those days when my sister and I would chase our little brother around the yard, playing, "I'm coming to get you," and running after him with our arms outstretched. He tried so hard to get away and we loved watching him stumble with his chubby legs. A little two-year-old he was. A cute thing too, portraying the characteristics of his father, our father. Daddy.

I always thought my daddy was a great father, based on what he did for my siblings and me. He was a mid-sized Jamaican, about 5ft 11 in tall. His voice was raspy, most likely a side effect of excessive smoking. He loved to laugh, and I can still hear the sound of my name rolling off his lips, 'Gracey.'

I remember those summer nights when he would blast amazing music from the reggae greats, Beres Hammond and Sanchez so loud, that the neighborhood lights would turn on, and behind the walls, we knew the neighbors were getting ready. The sound of lover's rock reggae boomed loudly through his mega speakers, and with the music playing, and sound effects accentuating the tunes; with the lights flashing and the disco ball lights rolling, we knew it was party time.

One by one, neighbors would come over with their hands empty, ready to receive. They were all aware that they needed to come with nothing because we had everything they would need. Neighbors would roll in, with a brief greeting to my mom, pretty much ignore us, and went over to Daddy. They navigated toward the cooler and grabbed their drink. Not just a Shirley temple, and no, not water either but a 'drink' 'drink'. I'm talking about Hennessey, Barcardi, and all kinds of rum. These drinks would cause an escalation in the volume of their voices and loosen everyone's mood. Man and woman would lock arms and sway gently to the beat of the music. It was quite a sight to see as a child. It looked comforting, I guess. I am not even sure, but I recall seeing couples holding each other close so that not even air could come between them. Some advanced to exchanging caressing and kissing, which I thought was weird. I wondered why Daddy allowed that to happen at the house. Nevertheless, it must have been OK if Daddy said OK, so, I would just sit back and imagine that being me someday. My father enjoyed these moments as he talked and laughed with his peers as he smoked away. Sometimes I would count how many cigarettes he lit a day. One time I counted up to 70.

As strong as the cigarette fumes were, it was no competition for the grand course meal that was laid out for all of us to enjoy. The perfectly squared potato salad, with its enriched tangy and spicy flavor, the zesty bread crumb laced mac and cheese, the crispy, honeyed fried chicken legs, and the crunchy cucumbers, grazed with a pinch of salt, from the garden sat on my plate in great anticipation of its devourment. I truly loved and cherished those moments.

These memories were so vivid, even though they seemed so surreal. As I reflect, sometimes I find it so hard to believe that it really happened. Life seemed so simple back then. Every year, my daddy would have a birthday celebration for me. I had a few friends that happened to be the neighbors' children, who would come over and celebrate. If the children came, then that meant their parents came, and if the parents came, that meant it was a party! Not just for me, but for the adults as well.

It worked out in my dad's favor because his birthday was so close to mine. We were indeed birthday buddies. He used the proximity of our birthdays to his advantage and would celebrate his birthday with his friends at the same time as mine. Daddy would have the place decked out from top to bottom, I mean balloons of all sorts, red, yellow, blue, green, and purple balloons lined along the yard, blowing in the warm summer winds. The streamers were meticulously braided, flying high on the stakes of the veranda. The yard was filled with the sweet aroma of rice and peas, steamed fish grazed with bell peppers and onions. Coca-Cola, Sprite, and Heineken stood within the hands reach of all the people who were present. The Heineken was off-limits to me and my friends. Everyone always had a great time when they came over to our house.

Looking back, it appeared to be a joyous time. I thought everything was as it should be. Our family seemed to be perfect. My mom appeared happy. She smiled quite often and seldom did I see her cry, but the truth was, while my mom was smiling on the outside, following my father's biding, she was dying on the inside. I did not understand at first, because you see, parents lie. Parents lie to their children in order to shield them from the pain of the truth. This is true partly because a child cannot understand, and the truth can be devastating. But if I am allowed to tell the ultimate truth, the lie digs the deeper grave because a lie can go so far until the truth starts to seep its way out. It oozes out, affecting everything in its path. Want to know the truth? My mom was living in agony. She was a walking skeleton, working around the clock to paint the facade that we called a happy life. She portrayed my father as the man, the kingly priest of our home for all the world to see, however, there was more to the story. More that I understood once the truth could no longer be held captive, and finally broke its way free.

Chapter 3: Today

A bout of nausea befell me as I felt the boat-like motion of my body as it rocked from side to side.

"Grace…Grace…Grace…" whispered Professor De Jesus as he gently nudged my shoulders.

My head sprung up, startled by his awakening. I almost threw up.

"Class is over. Are you OK? Your eyes were closed for the last twenty minutes of class."

The silhouette of a body started to fade and soon enough I was staring at this blurry-faced man who was intently looking at me. After several long blinks and a sip from my jug which now housed lukewarm water, I recognized that it was Professor De Jesus talking to me.

"Oh, I am so sorry." My face blushed red.

"I'm OK. Thank you, Professor De Jesus."

I stood up, legs shaking like a newborn fawn learning how to walk. I took a few wobbles and soon enough I gained my bearings. Eventually, I found my stride and gracefully exited the room as Professor De Jesus peered at me with great inquisition. It felt kind of weird and I could only imagine what was going through his head.

"Grace is awfully strange…"

Yea, that sounds about right. Maybe he could see right through me. I chuckled to myself and went on my way.

I sat outside as the brisk wind blew my curls across my face. The wind felt calm, and I closed my eyes as I nuzzled my face toward the wind's expression. Soon after, when she rested, I gently placed my curls behind my ear one by one then opened my notebook for another attempt to complete the assignment. I didn't know where to start, or how to connect my new thoughts with what I had already written down. I simply wrote these three words, "Who Am I?" I sat and stared at those three words and tried to find an answer.

The campus was pretty busy today. Students scurried back and forth.

There was a cute couple holding hands on the bench next to the student activity center while they engaged in an intense discussion. They looked madly in love. I remembered moments like that when I was growing up. As I reminisced about my romantic escapades, I happened to notice, not too far on the other side of the campus, a tall, geeky student tripped up the stairs. It was horrifying to watch as his books flew about six feet away from him, with his glasses not too far behind. I contemplated running over, even though it probably would have taken me four minutes to get there. Thankfully, a security officer was within arm's distance reach to assist him. I sat and watched it all like it was a movie screen right in front of my eyes. Hopefully, he will be OK.

I turned my attention back to my notebook. Every so often I would pick up my pen and touch its tip to the surface of my notebook, ready to write. Still, yet, nothing happened with my hands. Only three hours after class went by, and I was able to jot down about four sentences.

'Great!'

The day had gone by, and nothing was accomplished.

I scrambled up my books and sprinted to the car to retrieve my little munchkins from my mom's house before I got the warning call that I had expended my babysitting privileges for the day.

An array of white light shone brightly through my bedroom window. I pulled back the curtains for a clearer glimpse of nature's beautiful artwork. The stars played ring-around-the-Rosie with the moon, hand in hand. It was such a beautiful sight. Today was a long day and that scene was exactly what I needed to see. It calmed me and I felt a sense of peace.

After I picked up the kids from my mom, I brought them home, fed the little hooligans dinner, and gave them baths. I was completely depleted.

"Kids in bed…five little monkeys fast asleep."

I gracefully laid down on the bed, embracing my foam mattress's hug. I rolled toward the center, and hugged my knees into my chest, giving my back a good, long stretch. Markel had not yet arrived home, so the space on the bed was fully available. All for me. These quiet moments were the best. Once my husband came home, that serenity would end. This alone time afforded me the opportunity to reflect on my day and assess my feelings. These moments were priceless as they were few. Being a mother of five children was a full-time job! On top of that, I worked a full-time job and went to school part-time. Very often I found myself in awe that I was still considered a functional human being.

Most of my time was spent running around between work, class, and my mom's house, all in the name of catering to the needs of everyone else except for myself.

I closed my eyes and listened to the world outside of my window. The crickets conversed about their day, and the deer grazed quietly as they made their way through the rustling grass. The wind made her appearance every so often, and the trees danced in her presence. Nature was telling her story and I felt completely at peace.

That peace that I waited all day for, literally 8–10 hours of waiting, quickly came to an end as I heard the front door unlock. My heart began to beat a little bit faster, louder, and stronger as I prepared myself for the weird interaction that was about to take place. I heard the door close and the shuffling in the living room, providing evidence that Markel was indeed home. I stared at the ceiling and reflected on the inner sadness that had taken residence in my heart. Being lost in my thoughts, blinded me to the moans and groans of the staircase as he made his way up toward the bedroom. The door slowly opened and there he was standing with the plate of food in his hand that I left for him on the stove. I closed my eyes in woeful anticipation of his embrace. After placing his food down on the nightstand, he came close, and my body stiffened. He plastered a kiss on my cheek, and it was pasty. There was a storm in my heart that was raging wild, and it was becoming more and more difficult to weather it.

Chapter 4: Yesterday

The rain winds were fierce. I watched the trees pirouetting in the wind, branch-like arms waving to and fro. The raindrops formed diagonal streaks as they beat upon the pavement. It was storming outside, and it was storming inside my home as well. Mommy and Daddy were not the king and queen I had once thought them to be. All the wonderful, blissful moments that I perceived were a lie. The parties and partnership, the positivity and poise were all a lie! Deep within, there was so much hurt and pain that was exchanged between those two, and while they tried to shield us, they caused more damage. The pain endured was pain that we children fully never saw, pain that we were too young to understand, but Mommy knew. She knew of the pain, personally. She endured physical abuse from the man who was appointed to serve as her protector. She endured mental abuse, instead of being showered with praise for her true beauty and self-worth. She endured emotional abuse as she was forced to turn a blind eye to the other women who enjoyed the attention of her husband, fully disrespecting her and her position in the home. What other choice did she have? She had nothing of her own but was fully dependent on Daddy to provide for her the way he vowed to on the day they both said, "I do."

She forcefully took on the role of protector, as she shielded us, children, from the priest who was to guard the postern of our home and family. As the layers began to peel away, I saw that there truly was no happiness or peace.

The innocence that carried me through my early years ended abruptly. Only six, yet I became fully aware of the disharmony. I still remember seeing Daddy grab Mommy, holding her down as though she were a prisoner. My siblings and I stood there in awe, seeing this mighty warrior, whom we loved dearly, bring himself to the level of a filthy dog.

It felt like I was in a tug of war, better yet, a parent war with both parents pulling me, insisting that I shadow their being. My dad wanted me to side with him and my mom bid me to be on her side. While this was a no-brainer thought, my heart filled with conflict and contempt. Mommy's eyes filled with tears; her voice trembled like a sputtering engine. Daddy's stance remained strong and dominant, unaverred by fear or emotion. Thunder and lightning raged through our home, weaving from room to room. The rain of fear covered my body, I was wet. The fighting only got worse, and I knew the 'bliss' I had known all my life was coming to an end. The final fight was so ugly and we, the children, had to choose. Daddy kept calling for us to come and stay with him. He promised to care for us and love us the way a father has been called to do. My heart longed to hearken unto his voice, but my instinct told me otherwise. My little sister also stood torn, and my brother was too young to make a conscious decision. My dad became more enraged as he realized that control was slipping through the cracks of his fingers. He released his roar, hoping to incite fear, but fear already persisted. We were all already struck with fear.

Mommy called the police, and in the blink of an eye, the storm ended. Po-Po wasted no time arriving at our home. Maybe it was because we resided in the heart of the hood that the police arrived so promptly. The police advised my mom that it was best for her to leave the house. She needed to find a place to go, away from the unkind, unloving adversary. My mother did not once consider leaving her offspring behind. We gathered as much as we could take. My little arms could only hold so much. I turned to take a good look at the one who was called to be my protector, the one who called me his queen, the one whom I called father. I loved my daddy so much, even though he showed himself to be a monster under the mask. I really loved him. I realized that the heart of a child is pure and always willing to forgive the vilest foe, especially those close to their heart. My heart began to bleed. A river flowed from my eyes.

The night air was crisp and cold and we were escorted to the police car. The rain had temporarily subsided. We sat in the back, while Mommy sat in the front. The cage barrier between the front and back of the car confirmed my heart's state; imprisoned. I was stuck in my emotions and was unsure of how to process everything that had transpired. The car was flooded as our rivers of tears combined; our hearts were ripped out and torn to a million pieces. That was the end of Daddy. That was the end of our family. Even though we were physically removed from our father, it was he who actually packed up and moved out a long time ago. His abusive nature pushed my mother away. He instilled fear in her heart, causing her to close up and not live authentically. He stole her voice, and her freedom. I realized his chronic smoking and excessive drinking made him unfit. All of his addictions, anger, and need for control separated him from us. He left us to fend for ourselves.

Chapter 5: Today

"Good morning, Class. Hope you all had a stupendous night as you diligently worked on your final projects," exclaimed Professor De Jesus. The last time I heard the word *stupendous* I was a little girl watching Barney the dinosaur.

The class let out the biggest sigh, it was almost in unison as if it were rehearsed. My eyes simply hit the floor.

"Today we are going to take a break from discussing our assignments and instead we will conduct an assessment to identify our internal state," explained Professor De Jesus.

"Science teaches us that there are three states of being that we can flow between several times throughout the day. This can happen within an hour or even minutes. While we can readily flow between these states, it is a possibility that we could even find ourselves stuck in one particular state for an extended period of time. The first state is the shutdown state. This is the dark, lonely place characterized by feelings of numbness, and disconnectedness. An individual in this state typically would shut down and withdraw from the world. An individual in this state may be diagnosed with a form of depression. It could take one traumatic, stressful experience or many traumatic experiences to cause one to shut down completely. At this level, one may feel depressed, lonely, disconnected, numb, empty, and unmotivated. Simply put, pretty much a living dead."

Those words, '*A living dead*' were so familiar to me. My ears were attuned, and my eyes were fixated on Professor De Jesus's. This man was really dropping some serious knowledge on the class today. The very thing Professor De Jesus was explaining sounded so familiar to my ears, just like the sound of my babies' cries. I could attest to what he was saying on a personal level. Like a music track on repeat, all I could hear replaying in my head were Professor De Jesus's last words, "Pretty much a living dead…"

<u>Yesterday</u>

"Grace?" Janell's voice woke me out of my sleep.

"Yes?" I answered.

It was another evening at grandma's house, and I dozed off to sleep while watching an episode of the Simpsons. To be frank, now that I think about it, what business did a ten-year-old have watching the Simpsons? Anyhow, I did not mean to sleep at all. It was just a monotonous, boring evening, as was every evening at grandma's house.

My grandmother was in the kitchen cleaning up from the evening supper. My grandpa was sitting in his chair listening to my siblings chatter amongst themselves, and there I was falling sleep. Just as my eyes were closing, I heard Janell call for help from the bathroom.

"Can you grease my hair for me?" She asked in a yearning baby-like manner.

Janell was the mother of my uncle's two eldest sons. Even though they had these two children together, unfortunately, their union did not stand the test of time. I was not privy to the reason why their relationship did not work, as they were separated before I was born, but I always questioned that in my mind.

Janell had been busy washing her hair in the bathroom for what seemed like the past hour. Janell wasn't a fat woman, but she wasn't skinny either. Some would say she was somewhere right in the middle. She had a dark complexion, rich like chocolate, maybe even dark chocolate. Her eyes and teeth were white like her teeth were white like ivory, and when she smiled her eyes lit up. Maybe the drastic coloration was due to the darkness of her skin. She also had an award-winning smile. She wasn't the most beautiful woman, but her smile, I remember that smile. Her smile and personality were the keys to capturing a man's heart.

She had a huge scar, prominent on the right side of her mouth in the shape of an upside-down 'J'. The wound had left behind a raised marking, typically known as a keloid. That must have been a battle scar. I overheard her telling my cousin one day that she was cut with a knife when she was a child back in Jamaica.

Janell came to the United States on short notice after learning about the death of her oldest son. My cousin was only 17 years old at the time when he was brutally murdered in a gang-related incident. He wasn't even a part of the gang. Out of the goodness of his heart, he was trying to help a young girl who was being harassed by one of the gang members. Being a Good Samaritan and interfering in their business cost him his life. It was a very wretched time for my family.

Even though Janell wore a smile often, it was evident that sadness pervaded and won the battle. I remembered at the burial service; she was ready to be buried with her son. She man dived straight into the grave site hole on top of her son's casket and crazily sought to open it. The funeral directors and other family members had to wrestle her out of the grave hole.

It was evident that the loss of her son had a huge impact on her life and even though she seemed to be pressing onward, there was a sense of sadness and brokenness still visible.

After the funeral had passed, Janell did not go back to Jamaica as she was supposed to according to her visa. She stayed way beyond the point of permission. Being that she was a stranger in a foreign country, she had nothing of her own and was often found bouncing between family members' homes. During this time, she was spending some time with my grandmother.

Almost every night Janell would sit up with me, my sister, and my brother, and we would just talk, laugh, and watch scary movies on T.V. It was a habit that we developed together over a short period of time. While we should have been in bed, fast asleep for school the next day, we were creating memories. During the days and early evenings, she would take us to the corner store across the street and buy us all the candy that we wanted. She was so nice to us. Now that I think about it, it was probably her way of coping and dealing with the loss she experienced.

"Grace, can you grease my hair for me?" She asked again.

"OK," I replied nonchalantly.

I dragged myself over to the bathroom with my feet sliding and dragging against the floor. That sound was so annoying, but it continued anyway. I knocked on the bathroom door and she let me in. She closed the door behind me.

"Can you part my hair in sections and apply the grease on my scalp in a circular motion?" she asked.

Without verbal affirmation, I just started doing as she had asked me to do. I began to part Janell's hair and massaged the oil into her glistening scalp. It seemed as if her hair already had the grease that it needed, but whatever. I did what she asked me to do.

At the age of ten, doing my hair was my second nature. I had tons of dolls that had all these fancy hair styles done by me. I even had a doll, whose head was detached from her body. It was pretty freakish, but I didn't care. I threw the body away, but I kept her head because she had lots of hair for me to comb over and over and over again. I truthfully mean that doll had a full head of hair! Dolls nowadays aren't made with hair follicles on the whole head. Companies just make enough hair to give the allusion of a full head. You see the real deal when you unbraid the doll's hair and lift the hair to reveal the sides of the head. There you will find bald spots on both sides!

As I obediently massaged the grease into her scalp, I suddenly felt her hands pull me closer to her body.

"*Oh no,*" I whispered to myself.

I wasn't sure what to make of her sentimental touch. I started to feel a weird sense come over me. I was a little unsure of what was happening, but I knew enough to assume that I was in trouble.

She gradually started rubbing my buttocks and pulled me closer and closer. By this point, my 'bosom' was in her face. That was probably her objective. She continued, using her mouth to nuzzle open my shirt to fondle my little stubs. Using her pearly whites, she unbuttoned the top three buttons of my shirt.

"Oh, my gosh. What is she doing?" I quietly asked myself. I felt nervousness arise from within me and I did not know what to do. My mind began to race, and a funny, weird feeling wrapped around my body, and my mind. I felt warped and confused. My heart joined the race that my mind had already begun. I recognized that this was a sheer violation of my body and childhood innocence, but still, I stood there. Dumbfounded and stupefied.

Why didn't I yell or scream? Why didn't I just barge out of the bathroom and run to safety? I don't know. Was it fear that froze me in position? Was it embarrassment?

"Jan…" I shrieked.

She placed her fingers over my lips and pushed her fingers into my mouth for me to suck. Her salty, nasty, crusty fingers. It tasted like yesterday's potato chips.

My body started shaking uncontrollably. My mind was giving all the tips and pointers I needed to implement for safety but failed to effectively communicate them to my body.

I really wanted this to stop. I didn't want to do this and I didn't want to be here. I didn't know how to get out. Her foot blocked the bathroom door. I stood there imprisoned, and I felt warm tears running down the side of my face. My legs began to shake, and they felt wobbly. I no longer had the strength to hold myself anymore.

I screamed "*I want my mommy,*" but no words left my lips. Mommy always made things better. The tears ran down my face now, creating water stains on my white collared shirt.

Janell continued touching me in very intrusive ways. Her fingers maneuvered around the outside of my pants, touching and grabbing, rubbing and caressing. Even though I was only ten years old, I knew it was inappropriate. Why didn't I just yell at her to get off me? Why didn't I just slap her across the face and kick her in the gut? I don't know. I just stood there and let her have her way. Maybe I felt unworthy, and that I had no right to tell her what to do. Her hands began to unbutton my pants. Her hands slid inside my pants, and her fingers peered back at my underwear. She pushed my legs apart.

It felt like there was an excavator inside of me, digging, and searching for treasure. My body tensed up like an ice cube. She pushed her finger inside me which sent a jolt throughout my body. It felt like an electrical shock pulsating through every cell. I yelled out loud as she pulled her hands out and sucked her fingers off one at a time, as she stared at me with an eerie look.

I am falling.
I have fallen.
I am breaking!
I am broken.

The scream that escaped my lips was loud and piercing and it was evident that it brought attention to where we were. It was only a matter of seconds before I heard my grandmother on the other side of the prison door, banging it down with intensity. My old grandmother came in like a force to be reckoned with.

"What is going on in there?" Yelled my grandmother.

"Open this door right now!" she bellowed like a teenage schoolgirl.

The intensity of my grandmother's banging and the harshness of her voice shook Janell to the core. She pulled up my clothes as fast as she was able to and cracked the door just a tad. The next thing I knew my grandmother barged in like a woman with super strength and told me to get out of the bathroom, and she emphasized the word, now.

Grandma came to my rescue, yet she never said a word. There wasn't a moment of interrogation, there wasn't a thirst to see if I was OK, as there was clear evidence that I was not. She must have known something sinister, and evil was going on in that bathroom, but she kept it to herself and battled it in silence. I followed in her footsteps away from the bathroom and followed her example and never uttered a word about it either. Darkness fell like a blanket over my already shattered heart. From that moment forward, I felt a sense of anger and sadness toward my grandmother, and that experience affected my worldview. I saw people as untrustworthy. I experienced something that no child should ever have to go through, and it changed me forever.

Janell became a ghost after that night. The shock and embarrassment of her exposal must have been overbearing. She immediately left my grandmother's house and we never saw her again. My siblings would ask my grandmother about her. They missed her. But, for me, the sound of her name caused me to break down in tears and with devastating despondency.

Chapter 6: Yesterday

After my parents got divorced, the bubble that I lived in was broken. Life just seemed to flip a switch, and everything became harder. We had to move, and we no longer lived in that beautiful home in Jamaica, Queens. My mom didn't have that many options for places to move to and so we moved in with my aunt. My aunt resided in a huge home that she was renting at the time. I recall that it was big, but it was stamped with an eighteenth-century feel. I remember the bathroom tub standing on four legs that actually had toes!

The house was old, cold, and unfriendly. It was hollow and bore a sense of sadness, and loneliness as if it was not meant to be inhabited by humans. The main inhabitants were roaches! There were so many roaches that occupied that space that instead of running from them I decided to befriend them. I remember seeing one of them stuck on an oil pod in the frying pan sitting on the stove after my mom had made fried chicken for dinner. It was so disgusting.

My aunt lived in the downstairs section of the home, and we lived in the upstairs section. As cold, old, and sad as it was, we brought life to that home. My aunt had three children of her own, in all, there were a total of six children running in that place. We established many profound memories with our cousins.

Our once predictable routine had now turned upside down. My mom was able to secure a job as a United States Postal Service worker, which called for her to work at night. We went to school during the day but at night, my siblings and I would spend the nights at our grandparents' house which was just around the corner.

Things were so steely for my siblings and me. Life was mundane, almost rote, as we did the same thing every day. There was a lack of joy, besides the highlighted moments of goofing around with our cousins. Besides that, childhood felt so bleak, and life was no candy cane.

And then it happened.

There was a new man present in our lives. He was a tall, slender, Jamaican man. He was very handsome with dark, deep, powerful eyes. He had a beard that was well-shaven that filled the entire bottom portion of his face. His smile was like a burst of sunshine, and he was my mom's pot of gold at the end of her rainbow.

Would he be the one to turn our gray clouds into a sunshiny day? Would he serve as the new protector and priest of our home? Questions loomed in my mind as there was a sense of uncertainty that lurked overhead. My mom needed comfort and love, and this man seemed to fill the emptiness she felt. We didn't see him much, but just enough to know that he was someone significant. We began to see joy return to her smile and confidence flourish in her stance. She seemed happier and if she was happier that meant we would be too.

Life continued. My mom was working as a USPS worker, and she was dating this amazing person. He was so amazing that our family began to grow, all thanks to this new man! My mom was pregnant, and she gave birth to my little sister. She was a beautiful, chocolate baby, yummy to the tummy. Plump and sweet, she was, and I loved her. I loved her so much that I assumed the role of her personal bodyguard. No one could mess with her! Her smile truly lit up the room.

A year after her birth, my mother yielded forth another child. She was another beautiful little girl who was similar while simultaneously different, exotically different from her sister. She had straight black hair that waved alongside her tiny head. Her eyes were sleek and strong. They were bold. Her skin was fair, and she was a beautiful little girl with the physical features of an Asian child, yet she was born an African American.

My mom had not married this new man in her life, but after my second sister was born, it made sense for him to join us so that he could be an active part of this family that he contributed to creating. He joined us in our eighteenth-century home.

Not quite having the title of Daddy did not limit his ability to serve in that role. He felt like the dad that I was missing. We spent time with him and shared many great moments. Life started to feel joyful again. We did some traveling, where we went to theme parks such as Action Park and Rye Play land. I even remember us taking a trip to Maryland with him and my mom and we stopped at Roy Rogers to eat the fat-fried food they served there, which I loved at that time.

This man seemed to make my mother very happy. The tell-tale sign was the consistent smile plastered on my mom's face. This man in our lives treated us like we were his own. He accepted us, and his family also accepted us, so it was a done deal. He was more of a father to me than my real daddy was. Daddy. My daddy. Even as I write this, deep down inside, there is a never-ending longing for my daddy. I miss him.

To this day, I am unsure of all the details of the events that transpired, but my stepdad went away for some time. It was later understood that while he was away, he was imprisoned. He was caught and served time for a crime that he had committed prior to meeting my mom. My mom was faced with the choice to leave him there and after he served his term, he would have to go back to the place of his birth, or if she married him, he would have the right to stay in America, which would allow him to be with his family.

My mom chose the latter, and they eloped right there in prison. I am uncertain if it was out of love, or obligation. Regardless of her motives, I was so excited to feel love and warmth in my home. There initially seemed to be a sense of hope and renewal once my stepfather had been released from jail. However, it was not soon after his release that I noticed familiar patterns resurfacing.

After my stepfather came out of jail, things just didn't seem so right. He was incarcerated as a 'heathen' and came out as a righteous, and holy man, who seemed tyrannical in his implementation of religion. We were forced to observe the seventh day Sabbath which commenced from Friday at sunset to Saturday at sunset. We literally had to stop doing any form of work on Friday nights to observe this sacred day. There were times my HW was seized and discarded because I opted to break the law of the home. There were real consequences if we did not keep the Sabbath day holy.

You would think that if this holy man brought the spirit of God with him back from prison, the home would thrive on the tenets of love. However, my mother started to become dark, withdrawn, and depressed. She cried quite often and did not express any of her feelings aloud. I am not sure if she ever opened up to anyone! I was so confused at first as to what was causing her this despair, but soon we all realized that this 'holy' man was only holy in church. Once he got home from doing his servitude duties, my mom's knight in shining armor took off his mask and he was straight up a roaring lion, attacking from every angle.

It soon became obvious that my mom was being physically abused. Once that became evident, feelings of hate and contempt were conjured in my heart. I remember many nights when my mom was not at work, hearing her sobbing and whimpering in the bedroom behind locked doors. I tried to enter many times only to be met with it being locked and I was told to get away from the door and go find something to do. I needed to rescue my mom. What was he doing to her? Often, I would sit at the base with my ears plastered to the door trying to hear what was going on. Often, all I heard were the low whimpers of my mom's cries.

There was anger brewing in my heart, like a boiling pot of pumpkin soup. I just wanted to barge into the bedroom and beat up that mother F@#*&r to a pulp and pour the soup all over his face. I remember one time walking into the kitchen just to see my mom's arm in a twisted hold behind her back. She was crying and begging my stepfather to stop. One more inch upward and her arm would have been dislocated from the shoulder socket. Who the hell did he think he was? My anger was real, big, fierce, and powerful, but I was a small, incompetent, negligible child who had no voice.

Often, my stepdad's sister who lived with us at the time would bear witness to the abuse and jokingly tell him to stop but did nothing more than that. Soon, the abuse became more and more visible, and we could no longer deny it.

One day while my stepdad was 'man-handling' my mom like she was one of his old play buddies, I could no longer hold my tongue. I was enraged. My body temperature was at least 105.9 and I was blowing smoke from my pie hole. I boldly looked him in his eyes with fire fuming from my eyes, ears, and nose, and I blatantly told him to stop what he was doing to my mom or else I would call the cops and he would go to jail. Oh, my goodness! All hell broke loose! It is possible that hearing the words cop and jail triggered negative emotions. He immediately transformed into the Hulk, pulled the belt from around his waist, and beat me uncontrollably. He swung it north, south, east, and west. Welts immediately rose on my face, arms, stomach, and back as I tried to escape his fiery wrath. My mother eventually jumped on me as my blanket of protection and together we bore the pain of his anger. Despite the continual abuse…my mother stayed. Life went on. Our abuse became the daily norm.

Chapter 7: Today

"Alright class, welcome back. Please settle down, so we can delve into our task for today. So far, we have discussed one level of our emotional state, but before we continue with that discussion, I would like to get a sneak preview of where you all are with your projects. We only have one week left until we present our work," explained Professor De Jesus.

The chattering in the room started to increase as each student quietly asked one another how far along they were with their assignments. I looked around, then looked down seeking to avoid eye contact with anyone, lest I too gave an account.

"Each one of you will have a chance to tell us about where you come from and where you project the direction of your future," explained Professor De Jesus.

As each student took turns reading off their pages, sharing the story of their lives, I engaged in World War 3, or 4, maybe 5 within myself. What do I say? Where do I begin? Do I read all my notes? What do I omit? Question after question raced through my mind and the race ended when I heard Professor De Jesus call my name.

'Grace, it's your turn.'

I stood up.

My throat began to tighten and swallowing the golf-sized spit that accumulated in my mouth became rather difficult. My left eye started twitching, and I heard sleigh bells in my right ear. And no, it was not Christmas time.

"My name is Grace, and I am the oldest of six children. I come from a broken family, twice. I am married and I have five wonderful children. My family is perfect, and we are living happily ever after."

I stared at the class awaiting their response.

"Why are they looking at me so intently? Isn't that exactly what everyone wanted to hear?" I asked myself.

"Grace, are you OK?" asked Professor De Jesus.

I realized I had been standing there in a daze.

"You were standing there for about three minutes, and you haven't said a word. We are waiting for you to start. Do you need a moment?" asked Professor De Jesus.

Hesitantly I replied, "…OK…No…I am…um…ready…"

I began to tell my story.

"I come from a broken home."

I paused for a moment and stared off into space, transporting myself back to where it all began. The auditorium began to transform back to that 'wonderful' place I called home. The air in the room became thick like city smog in China and breathing became a chore. I began to smell the musk of alcohol in the air. Lung-corroding, earth-polluting smoke filled my nostrils. No one else seemed to be bothered. Just me.

"I grew up in a home where my dad was an alcoholic and a chronic smoker and he physically, emotionally, and mentally abused my mother. Night after night, he would drink and get drunk. Incapacitating words would escape his lips and race across the room, chasing my mother down the hall as she sought to relieve herself of my father's boisterous ways. This way of life was toxic and dangerous. My mother left him…and…and…it was a sad day."

I looked down at the ground to avoid any witnesses to my developing tears. The lump in my throat grew bigger.

"I really loved my dad, even though he wasn't all that I needed him to be. My dad used to call me his queen and that always made me feel bubbly and loved. Those words made me feel close to him. I wanted to make my daddy happy. I was his first girl child, so I always thought he had a special place for me in his heart. The day my mom decided that she had enough, and walked out on him, left an immense emptiness in my soul. An emptiness that needed to be filled."

"We left and we relocated to live with my aunt. Eventually, my mom met another man. Initially, he was everything that my father wasn't until he just wasn't good enough either. He too took advantage of my mom. He was physically abusive to her, and he was abusive to…"

Without any control, tears slowly streamed down my face and the words got stuck in the huge lump of saliva that refused to go down.

"To me, my experiences as a child created a love-seeking pattern within me that caused me to seek attention from boys, and eventually men."

There was darkness covering the room. The smoke had cleared but it was really dark, and the air was thicker than ever. Silence pervaded the room as every student stared intently at my tear-stained face. My lips, dry and chapped commenced to speak but Professor De Jesus cut me off.

"Grace, with the little that you've shared, I see that this is a difficult story for you to tell. I am proud to see the bravery exemplified by you allowing yourself to relive and endure these emotions as you share with the class. I would like you to finish telling your story in your assignment," said Professor De Jesus.

I sat in my seat. Slouched down into my chair. Saved by the tears. As soon as my body merged into the contour of the seat, the bell decided to ring, and we were dismissed from class for the day. I decided to make my way to a quiet place to complete this assignment.

The only option on campus was the library, so there I made my way. The library was a silent marketplace. Everyone had a focus and a purpose, and it seemed that nothing could have deterred them from their intention. It was so busy that I could hardly find a place to sit. I gazed around the room, scanning slowly and I noticed a small desk at the far back of the room. The area wasn't well-lit, which would explain the desolation, but it would have to suffice. I made my way over and sat. I opened my book and sought to resume where I left off while I stood in front of the class. I picked up my pen and started to write…

"My life continued on, but it was filled with an emptiness…a longing for more. I wanted to feel loved. My life was characterized by a false perception of love, and I

was yearning to connect with someone who could truly love me. As I grew into my teenage years, it was then I realized that the impact of my experiences followed me. It dictated the way that I thought, moved, and made decisions. My choices were rooted in my trauma. Truth is, regardless of how much I tried to mask my heart, I would find myself looking for love from men, hoping that someone would still want to be with a young girl like me. I found myself seeking to find someone who would love me and fill the missing void in my heart that erupted the day my dad walked out of my life. I began engaging in sexual relationships to please these men and fill the void present in my heart. I didn't want them to leave me, and I didn't want to be alone, so I did what was necessary to keep them. Even if it meant hurting myself. Even though it always proved itself to be unsuccessful, it was the only solution I knew, and it was the only solution I implemented time and time again. I was on a quest to find love that wouldn't hurt me, steal from me, or destroy me. In and out of relationships was my pattern, but eventually, I found my Prince..."

Chapter 8: Yesterday

Food, food, food. There was so much to eat, and boy did I eat. My stepfather's mother's house was filled with food to feed a nation. The sweet aroma of juicy brown stewed chicken marinating in cut potatoes, peppers, and onions, mouthwatering macaroni and cheese, and tender dark chocolate fudge brownies laced the hallway right outside into the backyard. There were also all kinds of rice. Black rice, white rice, rice and peas, and Spanish rice. This was a party, and I was ready to chow down. Out of all the food choices present, I chose to fill my plate with curry goat and white rice, and I ate to my heart's content. The food was delicious.

I spent a lot of time mingling with my siblings and cousins from my stepfather's side. As I was talking, laughing, and having a grand moment, it was only a matter of time before I noticed that something wasn't right with me. There was a tingling itch on my back that scratching could not soothe.

"These *jooking* mosquitoes!" I yelled in my Jamaican patois; an English dialect spoken by natives from the island of Jamaica.

While I scratched my back with vigor, the itching sensation sojourned to my arms and legs. My level of comfortability decreased as I tried to multitask satisfying the itch while chatting with my family. It only took one more intense itch pang that led me straight to the bathroom where I pulled my pants down and much to my surprise, I noticed that my skin had broken out with hives. I mean hives everywhere, all over my body. It was so sickening to look at and it gave me the heebie jeebies.

I called the house to tell Mommy what was going on with me and to ask her what to do, but she had already gone to work. My stepfather was there and gave permission for me to walk home alone and he would look at it. My legs were welted, and my arms and face were plastered with hives all over. All of this commenced after I ate the curry goat. What was in that thing anyways?

I made my way home as my stepfather's mother only lived two blocks away from our house. When I got home, my stepfather was horrified at the sight of my face and arms.

"Go take a shower and I will rub some Dettol on your skin to help with the welts," my stepfather said, perturbed at my appearance.

He had the right concoction to remedy every situation, as do most native Jamaicans. I did as he said, showered, dressed, and went to his room. He pulled out his 'medicine' and played doctor daddy. To make his doctoring easier, he needed me to take off my clothes so he could rub the Dettol all over my body.

I took off my shirt slowly and hesitantly. I felt weird and troubled by this occurrence. Even though my heart was stirred up, I shut myself up and trusted my stepfather would help me to feel better. I sat on the bed, and he began his work. His hands were so big and rough. My heart quivered.

I felt very uncomfortable as this brought back the horrid memory of Janell. She was such a pervert. I felt Janell's hands on me again. My heart began to speed, and anger commenced at the memory of what she had done to me. I was extremely tense, anxiety started to build, and I struggled to stay calm and relaxed. I had to remind myself over and over that it was OK.

"Grace, it is OK…Grace, it is OK…"

"Lay down."

I did as he said, exactly what an obedient child would do. He began to rub my legs with Dettol, an antiseptic liquid. He maneuvered up toward my stomach and he massaged the Dettol into my pores. Every squeeze on my limbs and trunk signified the love and care he had for me. He beckoned me to turn over and lay on my stomach. He pressed deeply into my back, running straight down toward my legs. After working the Dettol into my skin, he gently asked me to return to my back. He rubbed my arms, squeezing them in a circular motion. He went back to massaging my stomach, running both hands up the center, in between my breasts, then he massaged my neck. I lay with my eyes closed. This was a weird moment, but I knew it was for a good cause.

He paused, and I opened my eyes to see what had caused him to suspend his remedy. I was in a half-daze, trying to make sense of what was going on. He stood up and quietly made his way over to the door and closed it. I watched him reach up and bolt the lock on the top of the door, subsequently locking the bottom one as well.

He summoned me to turn over and lay on my stomach again. His tone was different, and the mood had changed.

The massaging resumed, starting at my neck, progressing to my upper back, middle back, and lower back, once again pressing deep into the curvature of my spine.

His hands made their way to my buttocks, which was the first touch of its kind. This touch was inappropriate, and I noticed my arm pits began to run water and my heartbeat intensified. This was a sexual kind of touch, one that was not expected. Round and round went his hands, touching me in a way that no longer felt therapeutic. Every squeeze sent an alarm to my brain and to my body, warning me that I was now in danger. In my mind, I saw myself pushing up from off the bed, thrusting my legs backward, like a buck kicking his arch nemesis, aiming for the groin. Before I could implement that plan into action, he took control. The pressure of his body consumed me as he plastered his lips on my body. He was hungry with an appetite that seemed insatiable. He ravenously parted my legs. He grabbed the jar of Vaseline and flicked the cover off.

My heart was now racing a million miles an hour. The knot in my stomach regurgitated into my throat and breathing became a chore. I was unsure of what was about to happen, even though I was smart enough to figure it out. Instinctually, the door was the goal. If I could find a way to hoist him off me, maybe I could escape. I couldn't get my legs to move. The strength I envisioned in my mind did not translate to my body. Execution failed.

There I laid. I wanted to call an S-O-S, but no sound could escape my mouth. My lips began to quiver relentlessly, and my legs were trembling. Using his index and middle fingers, he scooped a glob of Vaseline from the jar and lubricated my womanhood. I squinched my eyes so tight, and my body followed suit. He began to touch her and prepare her. He massaged her. Sharp pains radiated from deep within. I wanted him to stop.

"Stop I said stop!"

Why wasn't he listening? Oh, that was the voice inside my head. Not one word could escape my lips. Where was my mommy? Why was this happening? I felt so sick.

The weight of his body compressed me, and the heaviness of my heart buried me alive. I felt him enter and tore me apart.

I forgot to breathe.

His weight compressed the little air that remained. Reminded of my age and frailty, he was gentle at first. He broke me in like a new baseball glove, but eventually, he lost control of himself. With every stroke came radiating pain shooting up my back and down my legs. He tore me apart. He broke me. His weight sucked the breath out of my body. I still couldn't breathe.

"Mommy, help me…" were the only words I managed to whisper.

Tears gushed down my face like a streaming wild river. I wanted to live and fought to stay present with every gasp of air. Each breath was short and swift.

I cried.

I died.

I lost myself and I had no power.

I lay helpless, with the streams of tears continuing to flow. My chest was saturated with a compilation of sweat and tears. How did I end up here? Oh yes, it was all my fault. I should never have asked him to help me.

Soon the thrusting ceased, and his breath was heavy on the nape of my neck as he rested on me. My body still pressed down into the depths of the bed. I felt every coil of its springs pushing back up against me. Newton's third law of motion. I was swallowed by my emotions and confusion that I hadn't fully realized that he was finished. He rolled me over and pulled me up, bringing his face close to mine, fixating his gaze on me with intensity. I smelled the musk of his breath at the base of my nose and felt the bristles of his beard graze against my chin.

"If you open your mouth about this you will die!"

The aggression in his eyes was fiery and demonized. I no longer recognized this man. I stared at him until I stared right through him. I saw doubles and triples, and then my world went dark.

Every night I fell prey to his ravenous appetite. As soon as my mother went to work, and the house fell asleep, I knew my predator was coming. He was hungry and I was easy prey. Fear became my best friend, but fear wasn't good for me. Fear left me feeling exposed, naked, vulnerable, and depleted. My stepfather knew he could take advantage of me because I wouldn't say anything. I was just like my mother. I hid behind my pain. Suppressed my sorrow. I wore a mask.

Grief crushed and consumed me; practically stealing my voice and vigor. My spirit sunk low, and no one understood why. I sauntered around the house in fear for my life. I fell into a secret state of sadness and despair. To smile took an immense amount of effort, which I was always able to somehow muster up. My smile was my form of protection and if I smiled, no one would know or feel what I felt. I was unloved, unworthy, and deserving of what was happening to me.

This was what I needed to know and believe to accept the events of my life. It did not matter, and when I saw myself in the mirror, all I could see was an ugly black girl that was insignificant trash. Even though this was not a proper way for a child to live, it seemed to be proper for me. Even still I would often ask myself the question, "Why me?"

"Why did I have to endure this?"

"What did I do to deserve this?"

Chapter 9: Yesterday

I met Markel at church.

He was one of the cute ones. He was a musician, and he played the piano, and above all, he had dimples. Deep, crater-like dimples that seemed fake. Every smile he flashed caused my heart to flutter. Every girl would die to have a chance with that cat. He was a part of the 'in' crowd, one of the popular ones. He was known as the prince, in this royalty hierarchal system, the young people at the church set up for themelves. I was new, but I was privy to that information, as it was made clear to me that I was at the bottom of the barrel, the base of the totem pole, the scrapping at the bottom of the pot. I'm sure you get what I am saying. I was nobody.

There was a king, and a queen, as well as others of royalty. Me? I was classified as a peasant. Even though I was low in this hierarchy of young people, I had my eye on the prince. Prince Markel. Every time his hands grazed and glided across the white and black keys, there was an etching made in my heart. He saw me, and every so often he would flash me that smile! Oh yes, he saw me alright. He saw me as a nice girl, but I was obviously not his type. You see, I wasn't the epitome of beauty. I was plain looking. My hair was natural and in braids most of the time, whereas on the contrary, the ladies of royalty had perms, and their hair was long, straight, and beautiful. I was dark-skinned and being dark-skinned was not fancied amongst this group, unless you were male. I also wasn't a reflection of the world's accepted size. I was rather chubby and caused no twinkle in anyone's eyes. Nevertheless, I had an inner drive to pursue what I wanted. One of the ways I coped with inadequacy, and fill the void I quite often felt, was to go after what I wanted, and I wouldn't stop until I acquired it.

Can you believe that Markel and I eventually 'dated?' Our relationship consisted of playing basketball at my house almost every day during the summer months, hanging out occasionally around the neighborhood, riding our bikes to the park, and of course 'messing' around. We were doing things that my mom would not have approved of, but I really liked him a lot, and I saw that it kept him coming back, which I enjoyed and thought that I needed. I wanted to do whatever I needed to do to keep him liking me. I remember us stealing kisses and doing other forbidden things while we were supposed to be working at this Christian club, we were both employed. We were two crazy kids doing crazy things. Our relationship was elementary, but at 16 years old, attention was exactly what I craved.

Our relationship was pretty much a roller coaster ride…ups and downs.

It didn't make sense for us to be together, and Markel made that clear. Even though he spent time with me, and we had an informal 'title', he truthfully only saw me as a good friend. Once the summer days had ended and he went away to boarding school, there went that title. Despite the distance, we always remained close friends and we had each other's back for many years that persisted throughout high school and well into college.

During our college years, we both were engaged to be married to other people. My college experiences were nothing short of searching for love and for someone to be with. I could not fathom being alone. My fiancé at the time was good to me…sometimes, and other times, well, he was completely the opposite. I mean literally…bipolar? Probably. Unfortunately, that relationship did not end very well. While the engagement was experiencing some turbulence, there was additional interference. That interference was Markel!

He came back from college after ending an engagement with his college sweetheart. As we would always do when he came back from school, we would hang out and spend time together. Having common interests and tons of similarities made it so easy for us to flow together. The only difference this time with us hanging out was that he was here to stay. No more boarding schools or colleges. No more leaving. As time would allow, we started to realize that feelings from our childhood years were still active and after much contemplation on his part, we gave 'us' another shot.

Markel had a lot going on in his life, as he was searching for a career, and trying to find himself, and what he wanted to do. During that time, we seized every moment that we were able to spend time together. I recall going to the movies together, falling asleep on the beach together, and many intimate moments that we truthfully had no business engaging in. I was so fascinated with the idea of being in love and that someone wanted to be with me.

I was still in school finishing up my graduate degree, but I still made space for Markel. By that time, we had been officially dating for about a month and a half and I was so happy with how things were going until he shared something very dark with me in the form of a letter. Even to this day, I cringe at the thought of this happening.

Dear Grace,

How are you? I know that I am the last person you want to talk to right now. I am also sure that you are busy with your graduate work. I am so sorry, as I know that this letter will break your heart. I truly hope that you can forgive me. I need you to know what I have done, and how ashamed and sorry I am.

I have allowed my lustful desires for sex to cloud my judgment. I cheated on you, Grace. I am so sorry. This past week, I slept with my best friend's wife. It wasn't just one time, but it was several times throughout the week while I was there. I don't know what to do. I must tell my best friend what I've done, but I wanted to tell you first. They have their own family, and I just don't know how I let this happen. There's a possibility that she could also be pregnant. I am so sorry. Please don't leave me. I want to be with you. I know we are kind of new in our relationship but these last couple of weeks together have been great and I don't want to lose you. Can you please forgive me?
Love Markel

I put the letter down and decided to take a long walk to reflect on what had just been revealed to me. He had been working on a live-in job in the city, where he was renting a room from his best friend, his wife, and their two children. For the entire week, while his best friend was away, he shared many intimate moments with his wife, to the point where there was a possibility she was with a child. Not only did he break the friendship he and his boy shared, but he desecrated our relationship. My heart felt like stoned mush, full of anger and contempt, still yet saddened that I would no longer have a partner. He apologized and begged for my forgiveness, and as angry as I was, as disgusted as I was, as slighted as I felt, I stayed with him.

My life literally was dependent on this one decision, and I was blinded. Why didn't I just leave and walk away from him? I didn't believe that anyone else could love me. I did not believe that I was worthy of respect and true commitment but rather needed to be satisfied with what I had even though it wasn't the best for me. I was afraid of being alone and abandoned. The patterns my mother exhibited were rearing their vices and I fell prey.

He cried me a river and expressed immense sorrow for what he had done. His actions placed a wedge in his friendship with his best friend and distrust was born in my heart. Nevertheless, I stood by his side. At the end of the day, I did care for him.

While trust had waned, I was able to place the events in my emotional storage box and bury it back where it was hiding. I mean, I had to have a place to hold all the painful memories I have experienced in my life, right? Our relationship after that incident focused on our common interests which truly were music, singing, anything artsy, and church ministry. Common interests helped us walk on the same path and experience a sense of love and comradeship.

During this period of our relationship, we ministered in church and participated in all kinds of activities together. As a couple, many placed us on a high pedestal as they viewed us as strong leaders in the church, and in truth, that was what we were. We were a powerhouse couple leading out in music ministry, and youth ministry. But as we all know, even the best men fall, and there we went…boom!

Here we were, two young people, prestigious leaders in the church that so many other young people looked up to…pregnant. Having only been together officially for five months and having endured such a breach of trust in our relationship together, who would have expected there to be a seed yielded forth in my womb? Well, there was a seed that should not have been planted in my womb. I was too young for this, and I was not ready for the responsibilities that came along with this. I was still in school and had so much ahead of me to accomplish before I could even fathom raising a child. I was a baby having a baby!

I remember that moment so clearly. The moment when conception took place. The pressure from him to be intimate was so strong. Between having a weakness to resist carnal pleasure and not wanting to conjure feelings of rejection, I gave into his desires and went against what I truly wanted and felt was right for me at that time. He released himself when I told him not to and I knew that Plan B was the next option I had, but it came to no avail. Here I was…pregnant. What would my family say? How would this look in church? All these thoughts swarmed my mind. In order to mitigate the severity of the consequences our actions would cause, we decided that it would be best to get married.

While some were enthralled by our union, many others were leery and did not give their stamp of approval. Even the Pastor of the church reprimanded us for jumping into the huge responsibility of marriage without seeking consultation and guidance. Pregnancy was not a justification for us to elope. The Pastor made that very clear. I sat with his words, numbed by everything that had transpired. I really wanted everything to be good, OK, and happy feeling. I continued to add to my 'treasure' box of emotions, never allowing myself to process what was happening in my life. I kept reiterating that this was what I wanted, and I was truly happy with the choice I made.

Pregnancy is supposed to be a beautiful experience, but at that time it wasn't. Many turned their noses up toward me, judged me, and made me feel like I was the worst sinner in the world. Some of those individuals were of my own blood and kin. It was truly a challenging journey that I had to bear.

Markel and I faced many challenges as our baby grew inside my womb. We lived at my mom's house, and we were broke. Literally, we had no real money of our own. I did not have a secure job and neither did he. We were two kids having a kid. It was crazy. Many nights were spent in a pool of tears as I was unable to carry the emotional burden of my situation. I really sucked at expressing myself and what I truly felt during that time, so oftentimes, I felt isolated and alone. Understanding that line from the movie *Annie, 'You're never fully dressed without a smile,'* meant that I wore my smile day in and out even though it was the last thing I wanted to do.

The pregnancy had its ups and downs, but I made it to the end and we had our daughter. She was beautiful and I loved her so much. She came out of my womb flaunting two deep dimples, a mirror image of her father's. Her hair was straight with slight waves at the end and her skin fair and beautiful. Her eyes were radiant, and her smile was priceless. She was my world now. I somehow felt a revival in my spirit and purpose in my being. Her birth made the whole process worth it, and it afforded me a newfound purpose. Something outside of me that came from inside of me became my centripetal force. I could finally love someone with the love that I immensely longed for.

Markel and I faced new relational challenges having a child in the mix. We struggled with how to raise our child, what activities to participate in now that we had a child, and what things were OK and not OK to feed our child. Things were a bit rough, but thankfully, I had my mom to help me carry the load and made things easier for me. Despite her own responsibilities, this was her first grandchild, so she was happy to help. Markel and I managed to get through every day. We also faced disagreements about money, and time spent on unnecessary endeavors. Nevertheless, things appeared to be working. My fullest attention was given to my baby anyways and being engaged in common church work activities kept the wheels turning.

They say time flies when you're having fun, but I would beg to differ. Time will fly by any which way you look at it. As time would have it, my little princess was eighteen months, and I was pregnant again. I was so excited because

I really wanted my daughter to have a sibling close to her age that she could grow up with.

The beginning stages of the pregnancy were similar to my first pregnancy, so I began to speculate that maybe I was having another girl child. Thankfully, I had just hit the 12-week mark, and I was feeling a little more confident with sharing the news, I was more comfortable in my skin and feeling less sick. Thank God the excessive vomiting had ceased, and I was finally able to scarf down food without fear of regurgitation.

It was a Sunday afternoon, and my siblings and I were relaxing in the living room at my mom's house. We were talking, laughing, and singing some of our favorite tunes, truthfully, having a grand time. My little mama was touching something that I needed to take from her. I stood up to grab it from her, and the rambunctious room grew instantly silent. I heard the pin fall from my sister's hand.

"What happened?" I asked alarmingly, peering at the faces in the room, trying to gather some insight into the sudden silence.

My sister turned to me and said, "Grace, you're bleeding."

"There's blood all over your pants."

That was my pale, ghost-faced moment. I turned to Markel and said, "I need to go to the hospital…"

Chapter 10: Yesterday

I waited and waited. I still waited some more. Time seemed to stand still. My eyes must have checked the clock on the wall at least 50 times. All sorts of thoughts ran through my mind. I felt mentally exasperated. Gasping from a marathon that I had not yet finished running, much less begun. I felt hot and cold waves alternatively sweeping over my body. My mouth was comparable to the Sahara Desert. My mind was in a whirlwind and all I could think about was the safety of my unborn child. Markel reached for my hand and our fingers interlocked. I squeezed his hands as if life depended on it.

After what seemed like a year, the nurse called my name. She led me to a charcoal-gray room. There were three medium-sized paintings on the wall. One portrayed a beautiful ocean bed, with white sand, and birds soaring through an open blue sky. The other two were pictures of cute, smiling babies, one playing happily and freely, and the other sleeping like a sweet angel. As beautiful as they were, these pictures brought me no sense of hope or solace.

The air in the room was crisp. Cobwebs laced on the ceiling vents gently swayed to the cool air blowing through. I decided to keep on my sweater.

"Grace, please take off your sweater," charged the nurse.

"*Figures*," I mumbled to myself.

"Replace your garments with this hospital gown, making sure it is opened up toward the back," explained the nurse.

Her voice sounded like a low hum and was monotone and flat. There was absolutely no color or life in the way she spoke to me. She probably didn't like her job. Instinctually, I wanted to run out of the room, but my child's life was at stake. I needed to stay put.

"*Was my baby, OK? Was my baby going to die?*" I asked myself.

While we waited for the doctor, I decided to check in with Dr. Google to find an explanation for my bleeding and bring comfort to my worried heart. *What could be causing this?* I really wanted my baby. I had already loved it even though we had not exchanged gazes yet. Just because we had not met, this was still my baby and I loved it. Dr. Google offered more than 20 reasons providing some sort of validation as to why bleeding was normal at 12 and 1/2 weeks gestation. As I quickly read through them all, nothing brought me comfort or consolation, but rather increased my anxiety, as I tried to figure out which of the possible diagnoses could have been mine.

The real doctor came in shortly after I dismissed Dr. Google and the room instantly grew warm. Her smile caused peace to overcome me. Her eyes were bright, and she greeted me with a warm embrace. I instinctually laid my head on her shoulder.

She asked me to lie down on the table and to lift my gown. She squirted ultrasound gel on my stomach. The cold gel sent me into a semi-shock, but it was followed by anticipation as I awaited a view of my baby. The ultrasound probe glided smoothly over my stomach and then I heard it.

"Dub-dub…dub-dub…dub-dub."

The baby was alive! I turned and looked at the screen. There it was. My tiny, sweet, beautiful baby waving its tiny hands at me. It almost seemed as if the child was running to me for that 'mommy comfort'. Mommies always made things better. At least, that was my philosophy.

"Hi, baby. I love you. I can't wait to meet you soon." I gently whispered. That heartbeat was loud, and my baby was alive!

Chapter 11: Present Day

"Grace…I just don't understand. How can you say it's over?" asked Markel in desperation.

"I don't know. Markel, the truth is, I see you, I know that you are here, and I care about you, but I don't feel anything for you more than a friend," I replied nonchalantly.

My mind was gyrating. My heart was broken because now that I was practicing self-expression, I was hurting Markel by telling him the truth. For years, I have not been able to express my true feelings for fear of hurting him, but now, I was exercising that right.

Don't get me wrong, I have always cared about Markel and his well-being. I did love and care for him, but I was numb in every other way. There was no longer an intimate passion or desire for him. Agape love, check. Philia love, check. Erros love, Umm well. That was missing. We were live-in roommates who had children together. My life was literally on autopilot. Day in and day out, I went through the motions of life, until it started to kill me.

Seriously. My desire to participate in activities and events ceased. I lacked the motivation to do anything. The only reason I had to breathe each day was my children. This year the poophit the ceiling and it was everywhere. The clean-up isn't even worth attempting…or is it?

Chapter 12: Yesterday

A walking dead.

That was me.

I knew this state all too well. My stepfather did all that he could to buy my silence. I constantly received gifts, special attention, and privileges. I would endure the whining and cries from my siblings who were unafraid to express how unfair it was that I received everything I wanted but they couldn't. They did not understand the cost of my endowment. Being showered with the latest gadgets as a teenager would be a young girl's dream, but for me, it was the farthest thing from what I could have ever desired. It was a constant reminder of the secret that we shared. The secret I wanted to release and unload.

Not being able to release the burden on my heart cultivated a state of sadness and loneliness, and I needed to fill the void. I needed to feel loved. I yearned to be heard and seen. I spent many afternoons lying on my sister's bed staring out the window while listening to love songs. Those hours would be spent imagining that I was falling in love and being loved and cared for by the man of my dreams. I saw myself getting married and having lots of children someday. It was a strong desire that I had, and I longed for it to be filled every day.

Soon I noticed that other teenage boys started paying attention to me. The boys started to like me! I am sure part of that was because I lost all my baby fat and started paying attention to how I dressed and how my hair looked. I no longer wore 'do-do' braids as my sisters, and I called them which were simply put, big plaits in the hair. Now, I upgraded to wearing box braids, and eventually, I was able to perm my hair which made it permanently straight.

I engaged in relationships. These relationships started out with simply kissing. Kissing and caressing. I felt like 'he' loved me and cared about me by the way he kissed me and looked at me and by the way he made me feel. Eventually kissing wasn't enough and 'he' wanted more. I was taught from my abusive experiences that sex was what a man needed. Sex would make him happy. All I ever wanted to do was take care of a man and make him happy, so here was my opportunity.

Every relationship that I was a part of has had a sexual component. In my mind, I truly believed sex equated to love. They all said that they loved me. Was it because I was giving into their appetite? Even as I tell my story, I can't believe that I believed this lie that 'Love equated to sex.' How did that even make sense? I recall many moments of pleasing the men in my life. From behind the old building on the track and field area after school to empty bathroom stalls; sneaking in and sneaking out. We shared many adventurous moments. We could have been seen and caught, but I didn't care because he loved me.

I recall skipping school to spend the day with one of my boyfriends at that time. We had an all-day affair. The lavender scent permeated the room, lights dimmed, and music played softly. I was physically there, but my mind was asleep. I thought that being available in this manner would make him happy, so I made sure I showed up for him, but deep inside, I really didn't want to do this. In an effort to show up for him and give him what he wanted, I did not show up for myself and honor what I wanted. I knew I should have been at school. In my heart, I knew this whole ordeal was wrong, but when he smiled at me, all my thoughts disappeared. Someone loved me.

I recalled pulling that bathroom stunt another time in the men's bathroom during college. I was stealth…well, he snuck me in and out. That was a quickie, and I felt so disgusted with myself. God, I wish I could take it back. What the heck was I doing? I cringe at the thought of that moment. All I could think about was that someone loved me, and that mattered above all. I recall moments at my mom's house with him, at the other house and his house, and even his house. There were so many of them, and I am so embarrassed to admit that. I remember all the moments in my dorm room with him, in the car with the other him, and after church with the other him from the last time, before the first him.

I was a straight-up mess. Low self-esteem, low self-worth, multiple insecurities, feelings of inadequacy, feelings of being expendable, and unworthiness consumed me. I ate, drank, and lived these feelings every day.

Everyone saw me as this beautiful person, but I knew the real me. I was a monster, and it wasn't even my fault. I was ashamed and I couldn't face myself. The thought of all the things I had ever done haunted me daily. It caused me physical pain in my core. I hated myself for the choices I made. Choices connected to my past childhood, which were truly out of my control.

I lived in a home where abuse was the norm. My mother wore sadness and depression-like her daily apparel. She didn't know what to do. She had no one to reach out to. My mother's own childhood was loveless. Just seeing the way my grandparents interacted with my mom, it was evident that their expression of love toward her was exactly what she emulated toward her own children. It felt cold and distant. My poor mother. She suffered abuse from my father, and she suffered abuse from my stepfather. My mother didn't know how to love her children the way that we needed to be loved because she never received that love. We needed hugs, kisses, and words of affirmation. I needed hugs, kisses, and words of affirmation. My mother's love was expressed through provision. She worked what seemed like endless hours. Her love was maintaining a roof over our heads. Her love was ensuring that there was food on the table. A warm embrace or a simple 'I love you' was absent and apparently far from her capabilities at the time. It wasn't her fault and I forgive her for that. She didn't know how to give what she didn't receive.

The abuse at home was verbal, physical, and sexual. My stepfather was an unstoppable beast. Seeing my sisters butchered by his wrath would anger me. I was tired of him thinking that he could do what he wanted and that no one could stop him. He needed to be knocked off his high horse.

I wanted to tell my mother so badly what my stepfather had done to me. I started to pray to God that he would remove my stepfather from our house and that he never returned. The ironic thing was I had a deep struggle in my heart. Despite all that he had done to me, my mom, and my siblings, I still loved him and cared for him. As much as he angered me, I would not have liked to see harm befall him. God knew the struggle in my heart. When I compared my father to my stepfather, in a sense he had done way more for me.

One day, I witnessed my stepfather beating my little sister. His child, his own flesh and blood. He sat on her and whooped her so hard. The poor child gasped for air. My mom bawled hysterically, begging for him to get up off her child. She cried and implored him for the safety of her baby. I stood there and I felt so helpless. My face flushed with tears and initially, a sense of helplessness rose within me. Soon after, I felt that helplessness turns into rage. I was tired of seeing this monster in action. He needed to be put asunder and I would be the heroic savior to bring him to his demise! I had the secret weapon that would bring him to his knees. I was going to take back the control I relinquished to him so long ago. I was going to defend my family from his evil wrath. He could not have this much control over me or our lives any longer. If he was going to kill me, I was ready to go down with a fight!

I stood there and watched with my temper at boiling point. Finally, my stepfather ceased his torturous behavior and barricaded himself in the upstairs bedroom. My mom grabbed my sister and sat with her on the couch, wiping her tear-stained face-off, snots and all. I went and sat next to my mother and there were knots twisting in the soul of my stomach. I was about to tell her the darkest secret I had buried '6ft under'. I didn't even know where to begin. All I kept thinking was that 'she wouldn't, believe me,' I rehearsed the story in my head and marveled at how pathetic and unrealistic it sounded. Nevertheless, there was no turning back. I pushed aside my fear and embarrassment.

"Mommy, I have to tell you something."

"What, tell me?" She replied in stern anticipation, still regaining her composure after that frightening experience.

I stared at her with my mouth open, but no words came out. I didn't know what to say. I was so ashamed.

"Grace, what happened, tell me!" she yelled impatiently.

My eyes met hers and my lips began to tremble. The words finally escaped my lips followed by irrepressible tears.

"Mommy, he raped me. He abused me. He hurt me. I am so sorry. I couldn't tell you. He told me he would kill me if I told you, Mommy. I believed him. Mommy, I am so sorry. I didn't mean to keep this from you."

I continued to divulge words, some of which hardly made sense. My arms were shaking, my lips were quivering and tears streamed down my cheeks. Digging up this grave was one of the hardest things I had to do, but it relieved me. I sat in anticipation of her response. My mother stared at me in disbelief. Her eyes were filled with simultaneous pain and rage. She had no words, but it was evident that she was crushed and broken. She stared at me without blinking her eyes. Even though she was staring at me, she was apparently staring through me. She felt betrayed by the one she entrusted the care of her children too. I could see the pain plastered all over her face. There was also immeasurable guilt evident. I then realized she blamed herself for this.

Before my mother approached my stepfather, she immediately called his mother and told her everything that took place. My mother spared no details.

I could hear the high-pitched shrieks on the other side of the phone, and my mother rolled out the red carpet of shame. His mother cried imposter tears as I'd like to call them, as after all was said and done, she pronounced me a liar.

"He would never do something like that!" she exclaimed in defense of her son.

My step-grandmother could not keep the allegations to herself. She not only pronounced me a liar, but she called up her other daughters and sons and massacred my name. After the news spread like wildfire, my stepfather's sisters called our house, asking to speak to me. Hesitantly, I agreed to speak to them, and there was not one that had my defense. They all interrogated me, asking to hear the story from the horse's mouth. Even after I repeated the story again, I was deemed as a lying female dog…but they used the curse form of that word. My stepfather's nieces and nephews called me a liar and cowardly. I was barred from attending their homes and I was eschewed by his whole family. As if I wasn't already dealing with loneliness, the isolation in my life intensified and was debilitating to bear. Any lingering feelings of self-worth plummeted.

My mother approached and confronted my stepfather, face to face. I stood there by her side as she regurgitated everything, I had told her. He looked her straight in the eyes and said,

"Grace is a liar."

Regardless of his denial, my mother looked at me with love and compassion and assured me that she believed every word I had spoken.

It only took a day for the weight of guilt to become overbearing for his soul, because my stepfather came clean in the full confession of what he had done. His confession was intensified by extreme and belligerent crying. He apologized and begged for my forgiveness. Staring at him was the hardest thing for me to do. All I could do was cry. I cried for myself. I cried for him. I cried for my mom. He looked like a lost child who got caught red-handed. I looked at him and all I could feel for him was love and compassion. I felt bad for him. My mom and I were the only two witnesses to this confession, and he never admitted this to his family...ever. To this day, I am known as the lying female dog.

Chapter 13: Yesterday

The doctor checked all my vital signs and did a series of blood work to identify the cause of my bleeding. Markel and I sat there in anticipation, unsure of what news to expect. We hoped for the best but did not deny the fact that we could hear the worst. Markel tried to give me hope by offering words of encouragement. He quoted some scriptures, but I had a hard time digesting them and reflecting on that glimmer of hope he offered.

Markel and I engaged in small talk while awaiting news from the doctor when we were interrupted by the nurse who was taking care of me. Behind her presence came the cold wisp of air. I shuddered. She held a large needle in her hand.

"Is that for me?" I asked, startled by its size.

"Yes," she replied nonchalantly.

"Why do I need that?" I asked, as a matter of fact.

"You have Chlamydia, and you need this medication to cure you."

My eyeballs protruded from their sockets. I felt the heaviest pang in my gut. A weight load of fear grappled my heart. I took a huge gasp for air indicative of me holding my breath. She asked me to turn around and bend over so that she could give me the injection in my buttocks.

I bent over as she had asked me to do. I broke down right there on the bed and my soul fell out onto the floor. My brain sat on the counter, and I was just a body bending over, leaning on the bed. I never stepped out of this marriage and so it could only mean one thing…

Markel!

Chapter 14: Yesterday

"How could I have not seen the signs?" I asked myself, annoyed at the fact that I had been so naive.

"I can't believe he cheated on me and gave me Chlamydia."

I don't even understand why I was surprised about the cheating anyways! The glimmer of hope seeing my child bouncing around gave me a diminutive amount of strength. I sat up on the bed and waddled to the bathroom. My bladder felt like it was about to implode. I really had to pee, and I had been holding it for a long time. My legs were in pain, most likely an aftershock of the injection. I lifted my draping hospital gown and plopped on the toilet seat.

I was still profusely bleeding.

"God, help my baby to be OK." I silently muttered to myself.

I sat on the toilet to empty my bladder when there was a ball-sized object expelled into the toilet.

"Plop!"

It wasn't defecation. I looked in between my legs to investigate what foreign being escaped my body. In the bowl floated my 12-week-old baby bobbing in a grayish sac.

My world went black. I think I fainted…

Chapter 15: Present Day

"Good afternoon, Class," greeted Professor De Jesus.

"I hope that you all have been working diligently on your assignments. Today we will have a special guest visiting our class. His name is Dr. Price, and he specializes in the art of forgiveness."

My eyes lit up after that introduction.

"When an artist is about to embark upon a masterpiece, even though they don't have all the answers to their questions, there is a point of attention, a focal point. This is the place where they have decided to begin their flow. Most often, the path of completion is unknown, but as the masterpiece is created, they trust the process as their hands and hearts guide them to the finished product. The same is true for forgiveness. Without further due, here is Dr. Price."

"Hello, fellow students. My name is Dr. Price, and it is an honor to be here with you all today. Before we start, let me jump right in and tell you a little bit about me. My life has been characterized by bitterness and anger for the last five years. I've had to navigate loss beyond measure. My wife of 25 years decided that I wasn't good enough for her anymore. I have invested 20 of those married years, pursuing dreams and passions, all to give my wife the life and freedom she desired. Every dime I earned was poured back into my family. She decided that my sacrifice wasn't sufficient, and so she left me for another. My children lost respect for me at an early age because of the poison she planted in their minds. She defaced my character to them and to the world and I totally lost it. I lost my life, myself, and my being. I could no longer see deeply and even though I existed in the world, everything became superficial. I experienced difficulties establishing connections and relationships. Nothing mattered to me anymore. I got to a point where I was sinking deep in sadness and despair. My world became dark, distant, desolate, and destructive. I stopped caring about myself and pretty much life altogether. Following that, I had no desire to live."

The silence was utterly deafening. What a shocking and awakening introduction. Not one word was uttered, and you could literally hear a pin drop. Dr. Price continued.

"You see, I approached a fork in my life, and I had to make a choice as to whether I wanted to live or die. I am not referring to literal death or life, but my choice would have a direct bearing on that as well. I was headed left to my final demise when I came across a quote that changed my life. I would like to share that quote with you all today."

"Life. There are many things we can control, but there are more things we can't control. Knowing that, control what you can, and live."

"At that moment, I realized that I had no control over what transpired in the world around me. I had no control over what my ex-wife did or did not do. I had no control over what others thought of me. I realized that I had to make the choice to live. I couldn't allow myself to sink. I couldn't allow myself to commit mental, emotional, and ultimately physical suicide. It was time for me to start swimming. That's how I could control that! I realized that my choice would not afford me an easy path and that I was going to have to work diligently, step by step. Once I made that decision to swim, it was a decision to face the pain that had crushed me and sucked the life out of me. While we all have experienced different situations in life that have caused us pain, we all have that one thing in common: the pain," explained Dr. Price.

"Today we are going to learn how we can release that pain by facing that pain so that we can say goodbye to that pain and find joy, peace, meaning, and purpose in our lives. This will help us to embrace the art of forgiveness."

I adjusted my buttocks from the left to the right to alleviate the numbness I felt on one side. This man was my hero. There he stood with his heroic cape flailing behind him. Posed as one who boldly claimed his victory after a long, dark, stressful, but powerful battle.

"He has something that I need," I murmured to myself. My thoughts were interrupted as he continued to speak.

"Forgiveness is a lost art in today's day and age and because of that, anger rages strong in the hearts of men. Anger produces rage and that rage seeks revenge, and the vicious cycle never ends. But forgiveness. Forgiveness is the key to releasing the shackles of bondage. Forgiveness is not only for the offender, but it is meant to set you free as well. To forgive means to release the pain you feel and move on with your life where you can exercise complete control of your thoughts, feelings, and emotions. When you forgive, you reclaim yourself," explained Dr. Price.

Tears welled up in my eyes and quietly rolled down my cheeks. That salty savory taste filled my mouth and nasal cavity. The harder I tried to hold back my tears, the harder they fell.

Chapter 16: Yesterday

Sexually victimized at 10 years of age, raped at 13 years old, physically abused, mistreated, unloved, and unappreciated. This was what characterized my life, and it was truly a sad life. Now, the death of my unborn child was the new trauma added to the list of offenses that I had to endure. A trauma encircled by deception, infidelity, and selfishness. The death of this child was the price to pay for another's selfish deeds.

Even though I expressed seeing my child floating in the toilet bowl, the doctor decided to send me home to see what would happen over the next three days. They medical team did not want to deem the child a loss yet, but I already knew.

I couldn't understand why the doctor wanted to check on the baby to see if it was still viable. The image of my baby entering the watery grave invaded my mind. My baby. The baby I saw earlier on the sonogram monitor waving and jumping for joy. As I reflected on the image I saw on the monitor, I realized that the baby already knew. It knew what was about to happen and the dancing around was more of a goodbye. Maybe the baby was trying to communicate with me, to inform me of the danger that lurked ahead. Why didn't I understand? Why didn't I translate the baby's actions into words? Like, read between the kicks and punches. Coming back in three days was only to confirm what I had already known. I didn't even get a chance to say goodbye. No chance to kiss and hold this sweet child. This wounded my heart tremendously.

Even though I witnessed the loss, and knew the reality of the situation, I tried to maintain a sense of hope. I prayed to God for a miracle that my child could be alive. He resurrected Christ from the dead, so why couldn't he bring my baby back to life? Maybe what fell in the toilet was something else. It wasn't my baby. My baby was still alive inside of me. I adapted to a state of denial to get through those days. I made myself believe that life was still present in my womb. I spoke to my stomach. I told the baby how much I loved it. I prayed for my baby. My baby was with me.

Those were the longest three days of my life. Even though I had started to believe a lie, I was still burdened every day with true thoughts that my child may not be resurrected. I was haunted by the images of my husband sleeping with those slew of women, even some of which he did not know. I was appalled at the fact that he gave me an STD! What the heck! Who does that? Why would he be so careless and selfish? I thought he loved me and cared about me.

I should have pounced on his face for destroying me. I should have round-housed him and ended with a body slam, but instead, I didn't. I did nothing but cry. I cried like a big baby. I also swallowed the rest of the pain like a big pill. I buried my feelings, and it turned my heart cold as ice. I couldn't look at him. I don't even remember what happened during those three days of waiting. Did I eat breakfast? Did

I brush my teeth? Who took care of my child? Did I shower? I don't know! The days passed like a blur and before I knew it, it was time for me to face the judge and hear the final verdict.

Back at the doctor's office, there I sat in humble anticipation. The doctor I had initially seen at the hospital was off that day so I would have a new doctor. Missing the feelings of warmth and love made me miss her even more. She truly made me feel so much better.

This new doctor walked into the room. With my head still facing the ground, I noticed his feet were rather large. They looked like size 15. I slowly raised my eyes to meet his gaze. He was a Caucasian man, who looked about six feet tall. His face was flushed red, probably caused by sun exposure. Nevertheless, his face was warm and friendly. The look of sorrow in his eyes said it all as he handed me a sealed envelope. I carefully slid my fingers under the fold and took out the sonogram pictures.

The ultrasound revealed remnants of tissue sitting in my womb. There was no heartbeat. There was no life. My baby was dead and gone. I was in shock even though I already knew. The world felt so cold.

There I was walking alone in a distant forest. I was holding my little baby in my hand. It was swaddled tight, and I held it close to my chest. We simultaneously felt each other's heartbeat. It was beautiful. We were connected. As I walked through this desolate forest, I knew danger was lurking ahead. I felt it in the air. The winds howled and the trees shook. The trees were moving in a uniformed pattern. Their branches swayed left to right, left to right, rhythmically, and strategically. I huddled closer to my bundle and kept walking, swiftly, focused on reaching the exit to this horrid place. The trees became more belligerent, and their branches were hand-like. They kept reaching toward me. They wanted something from me. They were trying to grab my baby away from me. I started running now. I would not let them take it away. I wanted my baby. It's my baby! One branch caught hold of my baby's swaddling cloth and unraveled it. My baby was now exposed. "Leave my baby alone!" I shouted. Without a second to retaliate, the unseen tree around the bend snatched my baby from my hand.

"Give it back!" I yelled.

"Give me my baby back!"

"Give me my baby back!" I cried out with everything left within me.

The doctor took my hand and held it tight. I moaned and groaned. I bellowed over in excruciating pain. It was true. My baby was really gone. I was robbed. I peered out the window in time to see dark clouds simultaneously draw over the sun. Deep in the distance, I saw those trees swaying in the wind. I wrapped my arms around myself and cried. The cry continued to originate from the depths of my core. I continued to let out deep, ugly moans and groans. I banged my legs, I punched the walls. I pinched myself, hoping to wake up from this calloused dream. I rubbed my belly and talked to my belly. I screamed and asked the heavens, *"Why? Why me?"*

The doctor stood frozen out of respect for my pain and sorrow. He mourned with me even though he was trained to show minimal emotion. He continued to hold my hand and stayed with me for about 20 minutes as I released. His other duties were back seated, and he made me a priority. I needed that.

He hugged me with his eyes and his presence gave me a sense of comfort. After the intensity of my pain temporarily subsided, I stood up and the doctor asked me to sit down.

"Grace, we have to do a procedure called a D & C which is short for dilation and curettage," explained the doctor.

"It's a procedure where we go inside and clean out your uterus to make sure that there is no remaining tissue inside."

"Will it hurt?" I asked between silent tears.

"No, the anesthesiologist will put you to sleep. You won't feel a thing." He led me to another room and explained to me all the risks posed by the procedure, which seemed worse than the risks of not having the procedure done at all. The room was cold and smelled like antiseptic. The mist in the room grabbed my arms, and legs as I exposed them one by one in preparation for the D & C. I changed into the surgical gown and placed my head on the inclined bed and the anesthesiologist began his work. Before I could blink, my world caved in and I saw black.

The sky was dark, and the clouds loomed overhead. The trees stood as a dark shadow over me. Teasing, and jeering at my loss. The wind whispered to the trees and they kept on taunting and jeering more and more. I didn't want to be here. Nature has always been my place of refuge, but not today. I started walking away. I was angry. I walked faster and faster until eventually, I was running. The trees continued to stretch their arms forth and pushed me around like a pin ball. They took my baby and now they were messing with me! "What's happening here?"

Then I woke up and it was all done…in the blink of an eye.

Chapter 17: Yesterday

Things were a mess at home for a long time. Eventually, my stepfather ceased his voracious ways, but the house was still at war. My stepfather made it known that he was the H.N.I.C., which stood for the 'head nigga in charge' and whatever he said was the final rule. No one could contest him or refute what he decreed. Even though my mother was the sole bread winner, she had no jurisdiction over anything.

My stepfather had another daughter from a previous relationship, and even though we saw her occasionally, we were not fully acquainted with her. Unsure of the circumstances, our stepsister moved into the house one day. No warning or preparation. To top it all off, my mother did not have a say and was ordered to remain silent. Our already wild home of six children, now had seven.

This household was on fire and the head nigga in charge was the catalyst that kept the flames burning bright. There were nights when my stepfather held my mom hostage behind locked doors and all I could hear were her whimpers and cries. My heart sat lodged in my throat, and I fought back the urge to breakdown the door like He-man and rescue my mom. I remember seeing my stepfather hold my mom in a choke hold, similar to a move I've seen on World Wrestling Federation (WWF), now known as World

Wrestling Entertainment (WWE). I remember dodging flying cans, brushes, and combs that were targeted at the child who annoyed or irritated the beast.

With my stepsister in the fold, she became the newest target. She experienced beatings for all sorts of reasons, some of which included being rude or disrespectful, not getting a good report from school, or sometimes just because she looked like her mom.

At that time, I recall reading a novel entitled, *The Burning Bed*, which was an awesome book. It told the story of a battered wife who burned her husband's bed with him in it as vengeance for years of pain and physical abuse caused by him. Every page read reminded me of what I was living at home and many times I wish I had the courage to do what this young mother did to reclaim her freedom. It wasn't even my battle, but I was ready to put this war to an end.

My stepsister continually came to me for comfort. Her tear-stained face, pink like a rose freshly bloomed on her fair-skinned was her frequent portrayal. Anger had been birthed in her heart toward her father and she could no longer stand him. Many times I would spend precious time trying to unravel her flames, bringing her back to reality. Sometimes, all I knew how to do with her was say a prayer. I remember uttering these words to my unseen father up in heaven,

"Dear God, Please take my stepfather away. We don't deserve to live in a home like this. Please free us from his abuse. Amen."

No one knew what to really expect when my stepfather came around. It could be an 'OK' kind of day, where he was playful and jolly. Or it could be a 'bad' day where there was a hurricane brewing behind him as he passed through the room. The next 'bad' day we experienced was the new catalyst that brought about change that altered our lives forever.

The winds were violent, the furniture was shuddering, chairs were spiraling, and the curtains were dancing. There was a storm in our house and anyone in the vicinity of the tornado was destined to be taken down. Of course, my stepsister was the victim who experienced the full wrath of this vicious storm.

Like a roaring lion, he devoured his daughter. He sat on her with a whole 300 pounds and pinned her to the ground. She literally had to endure pounce after pounce from his heavy hands, like a lion devouring his prey. Her arm reached out toward me to make the rescue attempt, and there I stood frozen, in shock at what I was witnessing. I could not believe that this man would do such a thing. There was nothing I could do for her. I was horrified. Her cry was relentless, and her eyes pierced my soul. She was so scared. I was scared too because I knew that death was not far away. He said he would have killed me before, so I knew he was not to be messed with.

That night, after the storm had ended, my stepsister and I snuggled under our play tent. We spent many nights there sharing secrets or talking about boy crushes we had at school. Other times we would simply lay together and read our favorite books. That night, she confessed her complete disgust and hatred for her father and that she was going to kill 'that bastard'.

As much as I could relate to her anger and anguish, I refused to second that plan. Contrarily, I advised her to speak with a teacher or guidance counselor at school. That advice changed our lives forever.

Chapter 18: Yesterday

The lights were dim and blurry. I saw shadowed figures moving about me in a uniformed pattern. The world seemed gray, but eventually, it cleared. I finally remembered where I was. The doctor held my hand and sat me up.

"How do you feel Grace?" he asked.

"I think I am OK."

"Grace, you may feel unsteady and dazed for a couple of hours and you may also experience some nausea and vomiting. Please note that you may also have some light bleeding that can last for a couple of days. If you have any abnormal pain, please come back and see me," explained the doctor.

I nodded my head in a trance-like manner. I sat on the bed in a daze, as the reality continued to set in that I no longer had my baby.

Life no longer resided within me.

"You are free to leave," said the doctor.

My eyes met his and anger flooded my heart. Just like that…it was over. No more baby…and my life was left in shambles.

I called my mom and waited for her to come and pick me up.

Chapter 19: Yesterday

It was a Friday afternoon. I remember so vividly. It was 3 p.m. and there were 15 minutes left before the bell rang. I was looking forward to going home and watching my afternoon T.V. shows. I sat at the drums in band class, making up beats and singing some common gospel tunes that I knew from church. I was in my own little soapbox when two security guards entered the classroom. I didn't really pay them any attention. They wouldn't be there for me because I never did anything to get into trouble. I'm not being cocky, but the truth is, I was a good kid.

"We need to see Grace," said the security guard.

I looked up startled.

"Me?" I asked, giving them a side-eye stare.

"Yes, you." The guard replied as a matter of fact.

They told me to take all my belongings and follow them. We went to the main office where I met two adults who stood with their arms folded across their chests, embracing their clipboards as if their life depended on it. They both looked at me, and the young woman hugged me, pulling me close. My heart fluttered I was so confused. Why was this strange woman hugging me? That felt super weird. My own mother didn't hug me!

"What is going on here?" I asked.

"My name is Paula and this is Prance and we are both from the Agency of Child Protective services. Do you see that van outside? All your brothers and sisters are in that van, and we are taking you all away from your home…"

"…*away from your home. Away from your home.*" Those words resonated in my head. I stood there in disbelief, not sure whether I should be jumping for joy, or if I should be taking a dive in the river I started to cry. As the reality of the situation set in, I realized that this was more serious than I had initially understood. The water works continued with greater intention and pain. I just wanted to go home to my mommy. I didn't want to be held captive. I wanted to break free from Paula's embrace and escape to freedom. I felt like a trapped prisoner like I was being convicted of a crime that I was innocent of. It dawned on me that I wasn't just going to hop on the bus to go home. I was no longer in charge. I felt the glare of students as they rushed to their classes, some of them my friends. They looked just as confused as I was. Silent whispers flooded the hallways as we headed toward the exit of the school. I heard every word. Everyone followed me with their eyes as if I was some kind of entertainment for their thirsty minds as I was escorted out of the building to the van. This was going to be a long day.

Chapter 20: Yesterday

I never looked at Markel the same. I think I forgave him and didn't leave him physically, but a huge part of my love tank was immediately drained once I learned what he had done to me. I was working with 45%. I know that forgiveness means that you pardon the person for what they have done, but the pain I endured was etched in my heart and was interwoven into my DNA. I was disconnected some days, and on other days, I tried hard to push past my feelings and function like a normal wife. I spent a week living numb. Nothing mattered to me. I felt lost and my body's senses had all shut down. There was a carved-out void that I needed to be filled, and I was unequipped to handle it.

My heart felt like an empty room. There was nothing in it nor was there a purpose for it. I was incompetent in effectively expressing my feelings and the Jamaican culture I was raised in taught me to 'tough it out.' My mom and grandmother would simply say, "Hush, hush, hush." As a result of this reality, I dug another grave to bury my feelings and emotions so that no one would be able to experience my reality.

We started seeing a marriage counselor, who seemed to be interested in his monetary gain versus our marital growth. We went for a couple of sessions until we could no longer satisfy his financial appetite. It annoyed me that this therapist no longer made space to see us because we were unable to afford his payment. All I really wanted to do was to escape the pain I was experiencing and to see if our marriage could weather this storm. That was the objective of counseling. One of the things we were advised to do was walk through the process step by step. Unfortunately, I had a very difficult time taking that route. I couldn't endure the process of walking through it slowly and calmly as my form of healing. I couldn't wait to allow myself to heal mentally, emotionally, and physically from the loss of my child. I could not process my emotions as they were so overwhelming. I wanted my life to feel normal. I wanted my home to be normal and that meant I could not deal with the trauma at that time.

What better way to fill the void than to fill the void with another life. That was what we did. I was in haste to have a normal family and I really wanted another baby. I realized that I cheated myself of true healing. I cheated myself of the proper mourning. I cheated myself of the opportunity to make a clear and concise decision as to whether I really wanted to stay in the marriage or if leaving would offer me the greater benefit. I robbed myself of the chance to experience restoration. I sought immediate gratification and two months later I was pregnant again.

Chapter 21: Yesterday

At the van, I saw the gleeful faces of my siblings. I was fourteen at the time, and my younger siblings were twelve, ten, seven, six, and four, and my stepsister was in the mix too. They all looked so happy, sitting there in the van, and that made me cry even more because they had no idea what was going on. We were taken to the agency headquarters where our mom met us in tears. She was lamenting. She hugged my little brother, only four years old. My siblings didn't really understand the severity of the situation. It all seemed like fun to them as they were too young to understand, but I got it. We sat and waited around hoping to hear the good news that we would be going home that evening. I was optimistic and hopeful. Soon enough, we learned that we were not able to go back to our home. Our house was determined to be unsafe if my stepfather lived there. We were then given our temporary home assignments as we were being placed into foster care. The four girls were paired up and assigned to two different homes. My two brothers were paired up and sent to a different home. That left me alone. I was sent off to be by myself in the care of a total stranger. I understood that I was older, but why did I have to be alone? I always had to take the back seat. It wasn't fair. I am always alone! I am alone in my thoughts;

I am alone with my feelings and emotions! I couldn't believe that this was happening to us. I was petrified, but it didn't matter. I surveyed the room, zoning in on the faces of my siblings as they were sent off. At this point, the smiles had dissipated, and fear bled from their eyes. This was true of everyone except my four-year-old brother, who was happily eating a cookie. He was oblivious to what was going on. My heart was heavy and burdened. My mom's face reminded me of a canvas painted with sadness. What a burden to bear.

After we were assigned to our homes, we had to part from our mother.

My heart fell out of my chest, beating slowly, bouncing behind me as we were led away to the van to sojourn to the next destination. The pain was colossal and there was nothing I could do to escape it. We were all stashed in the van, and we waved goodbye to our mother. She stood there helpless, crying, and reaching out her arms to us. The van door was shut, and I heard the locks click in place. It was such a moment of finality. Panic set in and my throat began to tighten. I turned around, peering through the back window of the van, and there she was bent over in agonizing pain. My heart continued to slowly beat behind the van as we drove away.

It was a long ride to where we were all going to be fostered. The radio was playing bleak music, music that was complementary to the mood. Finally, an 'OK' song came on. It was Vanessa William's, 'Save the Best for Last.' The words made an imprint on my heart, and I let out the pain I felt in the form of raindrops from my eyes.

"Sometimes the snow falls down in June,

Sometimes the sun goes around the moon,

I see the passion in your eyes,

Sometimes it's all a big surprise..."

The words of the song had nothing to do with what I experiencing at that moment, but it was something about the piano and the strings that tugged at my heart. Her voice was so soothing and mellow. It made me want my mommy even more. I cried during the whole ride.

The night was cold, and the rainfall was heavy, both inside and outside of the van. No one said a word. All I could hear were the sobs and sniffles of my sisters subtly over the blaring music. We first stopped in Manhattan, where we were all examined by a physician to make sure that we were healthy and had no visible wounds.

After the checkup, my two brothers were going to be housed in Manhattan and the rest of us were being sent to Brooklyn. My little four-year-old brother waddled over to me, with his face hanging low. It was only a matter of time before he realized what was actually going on. He cried in my arms and asked me not to leave him. He hugged me so tight that it knocked all the wind out of me. I thought I would suffocate. Instead of trying to breathe in a lung full of air, I held onto him too. We embraced stillness. I rubbed his back in a circular motion and kissed his clammy forehead. The facility worker took him and went to give him a bath. He asked me to promise him that I would be there when he came out. How could I not give him that assurance? I made him that empty promise, just so he would go for his bath, but I knew I wouldn't be there. Every step he took away from me felt like a dagger to my heart. The tears streamed down my face as his eyes locked mine and he disappeared around the bend. I felt so helpless.

We all went our separate ways, with each of my siblings (stepsister included) paired up, and I was housed alone. When I got to the house where I was staying, I was greeted with the sweet aroma of Jasmine rice, or maybe it was basmati rice. I don't know, but all I can recall is that it smelled so good. My stomach cosigned with what my mind was thinking. My sadness turned to hunger, and I was ready to eat. I was taken to a small-sized bedroom that was big enough to fit a dresser and a twin-sized bunk bed. Someone else had already claimed the bottom bunk, so I guessed the top was mine.

I did not have much with me, as I had not been adequately forewarned of this 'vacation'. Somehow the aroma from the kitchen and the coziness of the room gave me a sense of comfort and safety. I hoped that my siblings were good.

Despite the peace, I felt, my life was silent at that moment. I tried to push out all my fears of never returning home. I turned my back on all desires of running away from my temporary abode. The first night was a difficult one, as I tried to silence my brain. I stared at the ceiling, looking into the darkness, wondering if this was real. I must have stayed up for most of the night because I was dead tired the next morning.

The sun shone through the satin red curtains and tapped me on my eyelids. I slowly opened them and panicked. I was unaware of where I was! After scanning the room, I slowly recalled all that had transpired the day before. My heart felt hollow. I lay there in silence, reflecting on all that had happened, and it was in utter disbelief. My soul groaned until my foster mom came into the room and gave me permission to travel independently to school, I became so enthralled. I was hoping that being able to go to school would afford me some familiarity and would give me a sense of normality in my life.

I went to school and pretended that nothing had happened. When those school mates who witnessed my exit bombed me with questions, I disclosed no information. After school ended that day, I called my mom before leaving and told her I was in Queens. She sounded much better; a bit revived I would say. She asked me to meet her at the family court. Taking public transportation had its advantages, as I knew exactly where that court was as it was a daily part of my 'scenic' view on the ride home from school every day.

Once I got to the court, I was unsure where I would find her, but soon enough, I spotted my short, petite mom, gazing at the crowds in pursuit of me. Once we made eye contact, my first instinct took control and I ran over to her. She caught me in a warm embrace. Instead of my mom pushing me away as was her wont, she held me so close. It was a picture-perfect moment that will always be imprinted in my mind.

After the hype of our reunion calmed down a bit, my mom told me that we would be able to come home in a couple of days. She was waiting for the final decree and the agency of protective services had to ensure that my stepfather had moved out of the premises. I saw the light at the end of the tunnel. I was elated and couldn't wait to be with my mom again.

Chapter 22: The Present

"Grace, I love you. I love you so much. All these years, I truly believed you were with me and understood me. I thought I understood you. I am so sorry." Cried Markel between gasps of air and silent tears.

I just looked at him. He was having difficulty grasping the revelation of my true feelings and emotions. I can't believe that I expressed how dead I felt in this relationship. This was so new for me and even though I felt incredibly guilty, I knew that this was necessary. I did feel the weight of his pain while simultaneously feeling minimal sadness and remorse. I felt sorry that he was blinded by his own distractions of life, work, and ministry. The thing that allegedly mattered most was slipping through his fingers. As I watched his tear-stained face, and quivering lips, feelings of sorrow rushed over me like a high tide. I felt sad for him, but I desired nothing more than friendship.

He couldn't accept that. That was not the way he wanted the story to end, and his stance made perfect sense. Here he had an 'imperfect' yet 'perfect' wife who held him up, even above herself. She saw to it that the family's needs were met and that everything in the home functioned properly. Every single meal was prepared by her 97% of the time. She took care of the kids in a hands-on way, every day. She bore everyone's burden in addition to her own. It made perfect sense that losing me was something he could not accept.

Unfortunately for him, He didn't have the power to make the choice for me. Day after day he would send endless text messages to my phone of prayers and confessions of his never-ending love. While he thought his efforts were making a dent in my heart, they only pushed me further away. I subconsciously struggled between feelings of anger and sadness. I was overwhelmed by his excessive tears and struggled with feelings of being smothered.

The next couple of months were some of the hardest to endure. Living a life full of obvious uncertainties was more than I could have ever imagined. No one knows the future, but to know that the future you thought you would have, was now coming to an end has created an inward surge of grief. I thrive on order, control and consistency, none of which my current situation afforded. Everything was in disarray.

Markel and I didn't get here overnight. We have danced in the mud for so long that it became the norm. We became desensitized by all the wrong that soon what was all wrong seemed to be right. The initial wound was inflicted at the time of multiple infidelities, getting an STD by his careless acts, and losing my second child. I was so wounded, but covered my gash with some gauze and medical tape and kept on living. I thought by suppressing the hurt and avoiding the pain that it would all go away. I thought that pretending that everything was OK would really make it OK. I thought that getting involved in various activities, and keeping myself engaged would help me. Unfortunately, the wound did not heal. I simply masked the symptoms with pain meds: children, church work, schoolwork, and everything else I engaged in. Now, I was infected; not just the initial wound, but my whole body was infected…sepsis has taken over and it became a matter of life or death.

Chapter 23: Yesterday

The years following the birth of our third child, after the tragic miscarriage of the second one, had some blissful moments. It wasn't always smooth, but we were sailing ahead. We started to make plans to purchase a home and we wanted to focus on building a better life for ourselves.

During this time Markel's father passed away, and his mom was not able to care for his younger siblings. Being the oldest, Markel felt led to assume responsibility for his siblings. As his family members deliberated on what would have been best, it was determined that a three-family home should be purchased where both families could reside together, and possibly rent out the third floor.

At the time we were already in the process of looking for a home for our own family, but my needs took a backseat. I put aside what I truly desired for the sake of what everyone else needed. I was truthfully nowhere capable of entertaining the idea of purchasing an extended family home, but Markel reassured me that purchasing this home would be best and that some of the funds left over from the life insurance policy would go to support the vision. Even though it wasn't what I authentically wanted, I went with the flow but made it clear that I didn't want to be directly involved. I understood that it was safer for me to stay out of the family 'politics'.

Everything was set in place. There was a three-family house available, and there were funds for the down payment, but there was a problem. Markel and his siblings did not have enough credit to secure the loan. I was adamant that I did not want to be involved. I was advised by many wise confidants not to get involved, and there I sat at the closing signing my name to a half-a-million-debt sentence for a three-family home.

What was I doing? I knew that if I didn't step up to the plate the loan would not have been secured. I deeply felt that Markel's family would look to place the blame on me. Maybe that wouldn't have been the case, but I just felt that I would have been the cause of this whole deal falling through if I didn't step up to the plate. I couldn't fathom the idea of being blamed and ostracized when I was already struggling with fitting in.

After the deal was done, I found every reason to make myself believe that it would be a great idea.

"We would help each other," I thought.

"The cousins would grow together," I explained to my alter ego.

It was starting to sound like something that would work, and I became somewhat complacent with the idea. Initially, things were smooth. We lived on the 1st floor, Markel's best friend and his wife (yes, the wife that he had an escapade with) lived on the 2nd floor, and Markel's brother and his family lived on the 3rd floor, so while we were together, I still had my space.

However, once we got settled in, I realized that an elephant had taken residence in my home. Having Markel's best friend there was a daily reminder of the infidelity that occurred between Markel and his best friend's wife. I struggled with 'forgive and forget' and the realities of what happened screamed at me every time she knocked on my door, or simply waved hello to me from the window.

We had some good moments and some rather uncomfortable ones. I was frequently horrified by the creaking of the ceiling above my head in the wee hours of the morning. It brought back flashbacks of what I envisioned transpired between her and Markel.

That elephant started to make a lot of noise in my house! Unspoken feelings, insecurities, jealousies, the constant comparisons…it was crazy how that elephant just took up residence in my space. I diligently tried to push past feelings of hurt and betrayal. Every day I got armored up, only to find myself defeated by the day's end. I was literally stuck in a comparison trap. She looked better than me, she had better hair than me, she was funnier than me, and she was lighter-skinned than me. She had something that I must have lacked, right? I was angry with her, broken by her, and still, I loved and cared for her. When I was with her, all I ever wanted to do was open my heart and give her a piece, but I was broken.

Markel's brother and family were higher up, but still, there were varying degrees of conflict when it came to the up keeping of the home. There were issues around finances, and it created great conflict within me. This internal struggle within me in turn did present some conflicts between me and the two floors above me. I wasn't always sure how to keep my world open while wanting to be closed. Even though this elephant was enough reason to flee from such a situation, I endured. It was a gruesome war within me, seeking to show love, patience, and forgiveness while simultaneously feeling hurt, angry, and betrayed. Church taught me so well how to suppress such feelings and love. Love is the answer! Yes, that is true, but it is often forgotten that love first starts with you. I didn't love myself enough to allow my feelings to be expressed, but rather suppressed and therefore, had to live with the stress of this mess. I could not contest what was taught but rather accept it to be true. I was told what to do, and that was what I did.

The elephant was growing and spilling over to other aspects of our lives. Things weren't flowing as smoothly as they once were, and slowly but surely things began to fall apart. Our issues weren't outright, but rather subtle. Once I opened my eyes and looked around, I realized that I was in the Markel family camp. It felt like they were all against me, even his best friend! We all had blatant differences that made it difficult for us to flow the way I had imagined. There was always a battle of some sort, order versus disorder, cleanliness versus uncleanliness, hot versus cold, dark-skinned versus light-skinned. My goodness!

The biggest issue of all was financial as it pertained to making the mortgage payment on time. I believed in paying for things on time as that is how you keep good credit. Timeliness over all was very important to me and just like our other battles, it wasn't a true priority for the other two familial inhabitants, even though they may beg to differ. I always believed that actions spoke louder than words…right? I would always make sure that we had our portion of the mortgage to pay on time, even if it meant denying myself some other needs temporarily. Unfortunately, they didn't share the same values. The mortgage was due, and Markel's best friend seemed to have the latest hook ups on his car and his brother just never seemed to have it. Everyone always seemed to be short on funds, but everything else seemed put together: hair, nails, foot gear…etc. I know that everyone has different priorities, so who am I to tell them what is most important? However, the differences in values made it very difficult for me to be who I wanted to be, so it was time for me to leave.

Chapter 24: Yesterday

After we returned home from our 'foster care' experience, life was a bit different. There was an unfamiliarity about our home. There was no longer a shadow lurking around the house. Fear was gone. There was a new visitor who sought to take habitation: Hello freedom! We were now free from the oppression to succumb to the demands of a selfish being. I should have been so happy. I should have been jumping for joy, doing cartwheels around the house. I should have been rejoicing, however, I felt depleted. I felt stripped. There was a void and emptiness in my life. I didn't have my father there to pick me up and cradle me in his arms when I felt sadness sneaking up on me like a thief in the night. I didn't have a way to empty myself of all the toxicity that had built up in my blood stream over the years. I cried physical tears, silent tears, and even mental tears. There was no one to rescue me.

I still longed to be loved, I longed to be valued and appreciated. I longed to be taken care of. That desire that I had deep within me was reflected in the way that I treated others. I've always been ready to love, give myself, and sacrifice for others. My longing for love cost me a great deal, as I engaged in a treacherous cycle. My body was desecrated, my mind debilitated and my heart was broken all in the name of love. Like Tina Turner said, "What's love got to do with it?"

Chapter 25: Present Day

"Good Morning class."

Professor De Jesus's sounded like clanging symbols in my ears. I never realized how loud he was.

"You have exactly one more week to complete your assignments. We will be starting our presentations after that."

My heart weighed a dozen grapefruits in a Walmart shopping bag, literally on the verge of breaking. I was nowhere near completing the assignment, even though I spent hours upon hours working on it. Digging up skeletons that were deeply buried was extremely difficult for me to endure. Many nights, eating and sleeping became an afterthought as I sought to unbury myself. I realized that my life was drowned by an immense sadness. I no longer had the desire to do anything. I was unmotivated, tired, drained, sad, and depressed. My relationships with others were strained and very superficial. I did not know how to be normal anymore. What was normal anyways? Was I ever normal? All I wanted was to feel normal. Markel's drive to win me back intensified. He became obsessed with being a 'better' man. He didn't want me to leave. He became 'crazy', 'stalkerish', and somewhat 'obsessive'. He started preaching to me day in and day out about God. Literally, everything was about God! He started reading prayer books, wanting me to join him. He overwhelmed me with text messages, notes, tears, and letters, all of which were to convince me of his love and that God would change everything around for the better. I heard him, and I know that God can do 'exceedingly and abundantly above all that we can ask or think' but there was no impact on me or my heart. Despite all his efforts, I felt lifeless toward him, and that is sad.

Experiencing a lack of love, and feelings of loneliness, betrayal, and emptiness placed me in a vulnerable position. I longed for attention. I wanted to be loved and I wanted to love. Markel's paranoia drove him temporarily mad, at least that is how I perceived it. His desperation to save us pushed me into a regrettable encounter, one that I am utterly ashamed of. I wanted to escape the pain; I didn't want to feel pain. I wanted to be relieved of the pain. I found myself succumbing to the call of another. It started out as a friendship; someone who listened and helped to fill the void space in my life. Our encounter provided me with moments of laughter, moments of feeling beautiful and special, and moments of feeling alive. The time and attention in that direction placed me in a compromising position that almost led me into a place of deep regret. Even though I did not fully compromise myself to the extent that I fell victim to Markel in the past, I was still wrong and felt the weight of my choices pressing heavily on my heart.

I humbly confessed to Markel what happened and while he was saddened by the news, his willingness to turn the other cheek was fueled by acknowledgment of his own past mistakes. At times, he would explain things to me in a way that made me feel that he viewed our mishaps on a comparable level, but in truth, while wrong is wrong, my mess up was a scrape compared to his gunshot wound that took a life…literally.

While he allegedly forgave me, he truthfully didn't let it go, but rather became even more obsessive. He wanted to know who I was texting or talking to all the time. He felt like I was hiding something. Truthfully, I was. I was hiding my true feelings from him. It was difficult for me to express myself to him for fear of hurting his feelings. I had a hard time being clear with him. Due to my inability to fully divulge to him for fear and possibly distrust, I found myself 'opening up' to others at varying levels to release what had built up inside of me. Whatever I did not get to verbally express was recorded in my journal.

His obsession became a serious problem when it got to the point where he snooped through my cellphone while I was asleep. Allegedly, he claimed he needed to use my cellphone as a flashlight to locate his lost phone from his car.

He woke me up out of my sleep around 3 a.m. with interrogative questions, asking me about the various conversations I had with my girlfriend about a guy I thought was handsome, and conversations with the boy across the street who made many attempts trying to hook up with me, which were not always clearly dismissed. I guess I liked the attention. Fortunately, I never engaged in any situations with this person.

I was livid that his paranoia allowed him to lose his senses and voice of reason. It caused him to invade my privacy. For all the reasons I had to snoop through his phone (late-night text messages, coming home ungodly hours of the morning, sometimes not even coming in until the next morning), I did not. I respected his privacy.

Markel was losing his grip.

Chapter 26: Yesterday

After moving out of the three-family house that I was responsible for, I thought things would get better with my in-laws and Markel's best friend. Instead, it took a turn for the worse. Our relationship was truly a silent killer. There were harsh, negative feelings that brewed around us, but words were never exchanged. We talked about each other to other people, discussing what we felt and how we were impacted by our living situation's demise. However, we never addressed this with each other. As for Markel's best friend, we each blamed the other for the failure but never took ownership of our roles in the fallout. I know I had not been perfect, and neither were they. We masked it all so well with cheap smiles and friendly gestures. The children between us all kept us glued together, as a somewhat functional entity.

After moving out, Markel and I functioned in a way that painted a false perception of our marriage to the world. In the church community, we looked like the stellar couple that everyone aspired to be like. I am sure that some envied our family. Little did they know…little did they know.

Markel was not open with me in the way that I needed and longed for. I really did want to try and reconnect after the multiple infidelities on his part, but unfortunately, he didn't know how, and I guess I didn't either. His life was characterized by accomplishing 101 tasks that always seemed to take precedence over me, even though he said he was doing it for me. We hardly saw each other, nor did we spend time together. Our time together was spent in 'church affairs': children's ministries, praise team, and choir rehearsals. My home was full of people, yet it was me, myself, and I.

I realized that even though I was married, I was lonely and began to seek outside friendships. I found myself connecting with old college buddies. Our conversations were innocent until they weren't. Conversations that lasted long enough would leave me longing and in a lustful state. Despite my growing desires, I've managed to maintain a level of integrity and respect for my home even though the struggle against that was real.

We rented another apartment for a while. We managed to function and were in a place of complacency. This was my life, and I had to accept it. After an amazing opportunity was presented to us to live in a whole house for the same rent that we paid for the apartment, we decided to move.

The move was a big ordeal for our family because that decision meant that we were leaving everything behind: our friends, our church family, jobs, familiarity, and a sense of peace due to comfort, for a whole new world. We left the city and decided to move to the country. This new world was somewhat scary because we did not know anyone. Nevertheless, we knew that this move was a blessing in disguise, and we were not to be fooled and pass it up.

We moved into a white colonial-style home on a beautiful, quiet block.

Tall, beautiful trees enshrouded the house, and it was truly decorated with nature's glory. Yellow, red, blue, and purple flowers pirouetted around the perimeter of our home. Each room in the house was double the size of our old apartment. The kitchen reflected an ivory antique-like feel, crafted like homes from the 1900s. Crown moldings gleamed off the dining room ceiling and the floors were a lustrous brown. There was an open staircase leading upstairs visible upon entering the house. The walls were a soft fuchsia pink, a color so prominent when accompanied by the glare of the sun. Each bedroom was warm and welcoming. I truly loved the new home. Markel and I started living with a sense of novelty and excitement. The change in the environment did something for us. It has awoken a sense of life in us. It was almost like a rebirth.

We hosted birthday parties, barbeques, game nights, and other social events. It was a perfect summer after moving there in early spring. We made new friends and invited old ones to be a part of our new world.

Once fall arrived, our excitement and vigor for a new life started to die with each falling leaf off the trees. The winter snow and cold brought her rapacious winds into our community and stormed right in through our front door. Winter took residence in every room and dominated our home. Markel and I became even more distant than before. There was a cold kind of love that existed between us. There were few words exchanged, little time spent together, and infrequent fulfillment of sexual desires. This was the resumed norm. To the outside world, we looked like a perfect family, but when the book was opened there was a different story. 'Never judge a book by its cover.'

Chapter 27: Present Day

Things didn't get better at home. They were steadily getting worse, as I no longer hid my discontentment. Markel's insecurities and paranoia drove me away. I was done but I didn't take that final step. We were pretty much living together on borrowed time. Every day was characterized by a facade. His presence made me so uncomfortable. The sound of his kiss on the children's foreheads made me want to hurl. Something was clearly wrong, and whatever it was repelled me from him. I think that I was frustrated with his physical absence, his mental absence, and his mindset that he could give 100% to 500 things. With each passing day, I knew that our marriage was slowly coming to an end.

Markel was working hard, planning all sorts of events for his job, as the holiday season was nearing. He was working late, not coming home some nights…pretty much what I was used to all the years we had been together. I was already mentally checked out, my body form silently moved throughout the encasing of the house, room to room completing daily duties and responsibilities.

Markel started to change a bit. He was still vocal about his 'undying' love for me, but he also seemed more distant. While I noticed, I chose to let it be. As Christmas neared, I spent the last 5% of my mental energy and vigor I had to decorate the house with some holiday cheer. The other 95% was expended on simply trying to stay afloat and present for my children.

As I previously mentioned, the holiday season was in gear and a part of Markel's job included hosting a series of concerts throughout the community. He was all over the place, running with different crowds; orchestrating different people from different places to accomplish his seasonal goal. I noticed however that there was a young lady that was a part of all his dealings. I didn't think it was anything more than what was visible to the naked eye, but I did make a mental note.

Thanksgiving concert—She was there. Winter Concert—She was there. Markel's car broke down and a ride was needed to and from the city—She was there. Church Awards Banquet—She was there. Jail holiday concert—She was there.

I saw a trend, but he said she was just a friend, and hey, what could I say? I had no proof of anything.

Even though I did my best to revive joy and bliss in the home by hanging up Christmas decorations, along with setting up our five-year-old plastic Christmas tree; sadness resided in my internal chambers. I just couldn't seem to find happiness. I was agitated and easily frustrated.

As was my yearly joy, I bought gifts for the family. I even included Markel, even though we were obviously not doing so well. Despite everything going on, I still cared and wanted him to have something to open on Christmas day.

Something about Christmas morning always created a sense of happiness and excitement. That was true for everyone except for me. I was feeling everything opposite of happiness and excitement. I was down and depleted. I had no desire to do anything that day, but I realized that I had to put the mask on for the children's sake. The children truly gave me a reason to push past my feelings. They were so happy and excited. I loved them so much and was willing to do anything to make this day a joyous occasion, even if it meant pretending one more time.

The children always knew how to bring a smile to my face. Many evenings leading up to Christmas day, I witnessed the children chattering amongst themselves, gathering old shoe boxes, tissue paper, and glue as they sat and made homemade gifts for each other. On that special day, with pride and joy, each child handed me their special, personalized gift with glee. Seeing their faces shining bright with joy, was a resurrection of my dead soul. I loved them.

I handed Markel his gift, and he looked rather surprised. He opened it slowly, probably confused that I would consider buying him a gift given the current state of our relationship. As he carefully unwrapped the present with anticipation, his countenance lit up once he realized that I had bought him something that he truly needed and valued. He concurrently looked at me with gratitude and sadness. I looked at him, and then at the empty tree, realizing that he did not take the time or effort to buy a Christmas gift for me.

Not receiving a gift from him felt a bit confusing. I didn't expect anything but at the same time, it was like a knockout punch to the gut. How could he be the same one professing his undying love for me but didn't even make an effort to buy me a gift? He could have bought me something from the dollar store! Just the fact that he bought me a gift would have made me feel a little special. But nope. He didn't even make me something.

To top it off, his good female friend, the friend that just happened to always be present at all his events knocked on the front door. I opened the door, and for the first time, I took a good long look at her. She was tall and very sleek and slender. Her squared face shape was revealed due to her hair being pulled up into a high ponytail. She was beautiful indeed. She greeted me and explained that she brought gifts for the kids. I couldn't understand why she felt obligated to bring gifts for my children. I looked at Markel baffled by her gesture, and he displayed a look of uncertainty as he received the gifts from her.

We all bade her thanks, and she was on her way. Markel handed the presents out to each child, and there was one left for him. Once again, there I stood…empty-handed. Christmas really sucked.

I did my best to stay focused on taking care of the kids and doing whatever I had to do to stand clear of depression, even though I was already self-diagnosed and warranted treatment.

On top of the holiday hustle and bustle, we received a certified letter in the mail from the landlord, informing us that we needed to move out of the house by the end of January. That only gave us a limited time to secure a new place, pack and move. Not only did I have to deal with life, the children, and my emotional baggage, I had to pack up a four-story house, pretty much by myself. I felt like I was drowning and there was no one there to save me.

Chapter 28: The Present

It was 1:48 a.m. and the chime of my phone woke me. It was a text message from an unfamiliar number. I rubbed my eyes, clearing away eye boogers just to be sure that I was seeing clearly.

"Is this Grace?"

"Who is this?" I replied annoyingly.

My heart became troubled, but after my question, I replied yes, without awaiting an answer. I sat up on the edge of the bed, feet barely touching the floor, awaiting a response from the mystery number. After ten minutes of staring at the illuminated screen, I saw black.

The next morning, I woke up and the first thing I did was check my phone to see if I received any further information as to the reason for the late-night text. There was nothing. It was a Sunday morning, a day that was filled with a long list of things to accomplish. My mind was easily shifted to attempt to be the successor over my duties. I woke the children up and set them straight to get ready for the day. I wanted today to be a relaxed day. We were so accustomed to running around town to various activities or simply running errands that I owed the children a day to simply relax. Heck! I owed it to myself!

The smell of scrambled tofu pervaded the kitchen. Morning star veggie strips baked in the oven at a warm temperature setting, as cream of wheat gently bubbled on the stove. Breakfast was ready. I called the children down, and like the sound of galloping racehorses, they charged to the dining table. The sound of them chittering afforded me a burst of sunlight on my habitual cloudy day.

"Today would be a good day," I thought to myself.

I made their plates, adding a colorful galore of mixed fruits: apples, oranges, bananas, strawberries, grapes, and blueberries. Surprisingly, I was really feeling good today. Finally, I sat down, with my plate gazing at me, calling me to take the first bite. As I picked up my fork to partake of a luscious strawberry, my phone chimed. Instead of going for the berry, I decided to see who it was. It was the mystery number.

"Your husband is sleeping with my girlfriend."

The room responded to the imprint of my face and the silence was deafening.

My heart sank and my head started to throb. This had to be a prank. I waited for the follow-up text. Maybe it was an early April's fool joke. I don't know. What was that about? I literally engaged in a self-imposed conversation. "This could not be true."

"He wouldn't do that to me again."

"But, what if he did?"

"No, he's not stupid."

There was a never-ending dialogue going on inside my brain. How could he have been holding another relationship, when he spent so much time working and trying to win me back? How did that even make sense? It was difficult for me to fathom, and I demanded proof.

The mystery man validated his claims, and it was then I knew I had to confront Markel. I couldn't wait for Markel to come home, so I called. Of course, he didn't answer, so I called again, and again and again. After the 5th attempt, he picked up the phone.

Without a proper greeting, I just hit the nail on the head.

"Markel, I was just told you were having an affair with your friend?"

He replied unsure of which friend I was referring to. Just to be sure he clearly understood what I was saying, I continued to clarify.

"The girl that has been helping you a lot with your work and stuff, the girl who brought all the gifts for you and the kids…that girl."

Markel's silence on the other end of the phone sounded like the silence of a child who was caught red-handed stealing cookies from the cookie jar.

"Tell me if this is true!" I demanded.

"Grace, I can explain."

"Just tell me if it is true!" I shouted.

"Yes. It is true."

His response sounded like he had his head cropped between his legs like a shameful dog. I hung up the phone and placed my hands over my tightly shut eyes. My head began to spin, and I suddenly felt weak as I remembered seeing my baby in the sonogram bouncing around, waving at me. Little did I know, but it was crying out for help…to be rescued before it landed in its watery toilet grave. Maybe the baby was warning me to get out of the marriage then, trying to spare me the pain. I remembered learning of all the women he had been with. I remember feeling betrayed. The air around me grew thick, and each breath became more and more challenging to execute. I could no longer take a breath. I rushed to the window and let in the cold, blustery air. I closed my eyes and started to take deep, long breaths.

My world had stood still. Even though things were clearly done on my end, there was a sense of betrayal that culminated within me. I wanted to know more. I needed to know more details.

I had to beg and dig to learn more about what transpired between them. My intuition was correct. The same girl I suspiciously had my eyes on was the same one who had her eye on Markel. He must have had his eye on her too. They were straight up in it together. I learned that it wasn't just a simple one-time mistake, but rather a conscious decision to engage in an emotional, mental and physical relationship with her. It wasn't just one time that could convincingly be a mistake. There was a purposeful decision. Adequate thought and planning were put into what they built. He was messing with her for three months while still trying to be with me.

Moments when she was around, she was all up in his world and I sat right there, looking like the dumb, blind wife. I learned a lot from the mystery man about their dealings. Markel tried to keep me in the dark about the details. He wasn't even the one who spilled the beans. It made me wonder if he would have ever told me if I never found out the way I did. Markel disrespected our marriage on a whole other level.

He didn't just have sex with her, he made love to her. The thought of that reality destroyed me again. What made this matter worse is that he desecrated our very own bed! That was the lowest he had ever gone. That decision was a deliberate act of betrayal with little to no regard for the consequences, and how it would be the official end of our marriage.

Markel expected me to forgive him, and he wanted to continue his fight to save and restore our marriage. Unfortunately, I don't think he realized that he was the one that ended our marriage. Even though I was done, I never physically walked away. The day that he made love to her on my bed, on my sheets that I slept on, laying on my pillow, in my space was the day he kissed our union goodbye.

The relationship had come to an end. I think I forgave him but was no longer going to allow my feelings to be held captive any longer. My heart was telling me the truth all along, but I didn't trust it. I didn't trust myself enough. I always doubted myself but believed everything everyone else said. My voice was hushed, and the world dictated my life.

No more.

No more would I allow me to fall prey to the ideologies of others. It was my life, and I was responsible for what happened to me because of the choices I made. If I drowned in misery, it was my fault, because I chose to stay there. If I succeeded, it was because of the choices I made.

So, what will I do now?

I decided to get a divorce. This was a hard decision for me to make, not because I wasn't sure, but because I knew the sadness it would bring to my children. I didn't want to hurt my babies. I knew of the hurt and pain that came along with divorce all too well. I wanted to protect them, but I realized that living a lie would be even more damaging to them. From this incident, I taught my children about the consequences of disobedience. I reminded them daily that there is a price to pay when we disobey.

What a fitting time for all this to transpire. We needed to vacate the house, and for the first time since the birth of my first child, I would be moving without a husband. The divorce process has been physically, mentally, and emotionally taxing on me. The task of mothering and working, and schooling while dealing with everything has pressed me down to the point where I have lost all feeling.

With permission granted to exit the marriage, I wasted no time delving into the divorce proceedings. I contacted a lawyer and followed through with everything that needed to be done. I vowed to myself that despite what happened between Markel and me, I would do whatever I needed to do to ensure that my kids always had access to their dad. The process was gruesome, and I was met with some resistance. However, despite the journey, I did not lose sight of the goal-freedom.

Chapter 29: The Present

Life after the divorce was not a walk in the park. It was a journey of reflection, loneliness, guilt, shame, defending, teaching, and sharing. Time had elapsed, and approximately six months had passed since the divorce. I appreciated the freedom, even though I was saddened by the loneliness. I was always lonely, but this time the loneliness was stronger. I wanted to be married again. I felt deep within the core of my bones that I was not meant to be alone. Regardless of what I wanted; marriage was far off for me.

I was on a journey. A road to experience the healing that was due to me since my childhood. I had to stay on the course and not let any fleeting feelings or raging hormones distract me from what I needed to accomplish. I needed to keep my eyes off anything or anyone that would deter me from what I needed to accomplish.

And then I met him.

It was a warm spring afternoon, and I was running into Dominoes to pick up a pizza pie I ordered for my ravenous birds. I was in a rush and tried intensely to maintain a patient posture even though I was a ticking time bomb ready to explode out of there. The manager seemed to be moving around like a chicken without a head. He came to the front to take orders, he moved to the back to put a pie in the oven, he gave orders to the worker on the left to restack the boxes as they had fallen over, and he went ahead and helped stack boxes on the right. Oh, man! I just wanted my pizza!

He was tall and slender. His clothes were fit enough for me to see the contour of his masculinity. He wore a hat that covered his eyes, but his smile was bright. He was dark chocolate, and not too bad on the eyes, but I wasn't too focused on him anyways.

After what seemed like a decade, he finally brought the large pie over and apologized for its delay. As he rang up my order, he decided to play into the moment with small talk.

"Running late to a meeting at work?" he asked.

"No," I replied, "Just getting some food for my children."

"What? Children? You don't look a day over 25 years old."

A way to a woman's heart is to tell her she looks younger than she really is. I smiled. Those words softened my stance and I let my guard down a bit. He stared intently at me as I smiled and there was some unspoken exchange of emotions that transpired between the both of us. I could tell that he liked my smile.

He mustered up the courage to tell me amidst all the hustle and bustle of pizza making, that he thought I was beautiful.

"I would love to chat some more later, maybe take you out to dinner."

He paused and we stared at each other with awkward silence dancing around us while the store continued to bustle with excitement.

"Can I have your number?" he asked.

With a conflict brewing in my heart and knowing that I really did not have time for this, I quickly scribbled my number on a piece of paper that he handed me and dashed out the door, gleefully.

I felt beautiful and desired. I was happy that someone could still look at me and see value and worth. I was amazed that I could still be 'chased' and that I still 'had it'. The rest of my day whizzed by and the moment I subconsciously anticipated had arrived.

He called me that evening, and we had a beautiful conversation. We spent a great deal of time on the phone, after I put my kids to bed, learning about his background. He had a story to tell, as I learned of the hardships of his childhood and the treacherous ways of his family. I too openly shared my historical endeavors, and he listened intently. He seemed to empathize with me as I shared. We had a magnetic connection and my desire to learn more about him was intense.

It's strange to admit that even though I had not been single for that long after having been in a long-term relationship, I felt a genuine connection. We talked for 4–5 hours daily. I felt like I knew him forever. I still wanted to know more and experience more. I was hungry, thirsty, and craving for more. After a week of building the blocks of our friendship foundation, he asked me out on a date. I remember the flips and turns that happened in my stomach. I was so excited but nervous at the same time. All I could think about was how I would have behaved. I had not been on a date in a very long time! I looked forward to our meeting and I did everything I could to ensure that I was available to go.

He took me out to a restaurant, where we ate until our bellies overflowed. To top it off, we shared a double chocolate mousse cake. We talked, laughed, hugged, and even shared a kiss. That date was the start of something magical. I was falling in love.

We continued to talk for endless hours, multiple times a day about a plethora of things. There was so much more to learn. We talked about the future together. We planned on buying a house in Tennessee, and we wanted to have three children, which would mean I would have eight. He would often visit me during his lunch breaks, and we would eat pizza together. (Hey, it was free and good!) This young man had given me a new vitality for living. I was ready to love again.

Chapter 30: Present Day

I was so blinded by that love, I failed to see some of the red flags being waved in my face. He knew where I lived and spent many hours at my home, but he never once invited me to his home. Many times, he needed me to run errands for him and I would sacrifice a great deal to ensure that I granted whatever he desired, but seldom to none did he do the same for me. My requests were often met with excuses or downright resistance.

Nonetheless, I loved him. He made me happy, and he made me feel good emotionally and above all, physically. Six months into our dating, he told me that he needed to get away. He was taking a trip and would be unavailable to speak with me, so I need not call or try to reach out to him. I was so confused about that notion, and it made no sense. You don't just disappear and tell your girlfriend not to call you! For one whole week, he was gone. I missed him like crazy. I missed our talks and moments when we spent time together. I missed his strong embrace, the way he rubbed my back and held my hand. I couldn't focus, the quality of my mothering diminished, and my work performance was weakened.

He pretty much ghosted me in a nice way. Not having forewarning as to when the ghosting would end, on the 8th day he reached out to me and told me how much he missed me. My heart embraced his words with utmost joy and glee. I was so happy again. After pouring his sweet words of affirmation into my ears, the ghosting period ended because he needed me again. He needed me to do a huge favor for him, one that would disrupt the flow of my day, but I was willing to sacrifice, and do it because it was him! The love of my life.

Every morning, I woke up at the crack of dawn, packed up my children, and headed to the area where he lived, which was about 60 miles away to pick him up at the local Dunkin shop. He needed me to drive him all the way back to where I lived and he worked so that he could get there as his car had been seized by the police due to speeding on the highway. At the end of the day, I took him back home after I was done with work.

Love makes you do all kinds of crazy things and that is what I did. I did whatever he needed me to do. Our time together was thrilling and wild, and I was always there when he needed me.

Chapter 31: The Present

It had been five days since my cycle was to start and still nothing. While I tried my best to believe otherwise, I knew exactly what was up. I knew I needed to take a test to validate what I had been suspecting since day one of Aunt Flow's absence. Once I confirmed my suspicions, I pulled out my phone and eagerly shot over a quick text to my other half.

"Babe, we're having a baby."

The excitement started to brew in my heart as the countless conversations we shared about starting a family came flooding back into my mind. This was going to be a fulfillment of what he had spoken of.

I continued to wait for the ping on my phone, but it never came.

Ten minutes had passed and I did not hear from him. Assuming it was hectic at the shop, I decided to call. After three attempts, he finally answered. I shared the great news and sat awaited expectantly to hear a burst of excitement come through the phone and embrace my heart, but instead, there was a dead silence.

"Hello?" I asked.

I thought maybe we had gotten disconnected.

He responded in the affirmative and then my heart began to bow.

"Babe, did you hear the news I just shared?" I asked again hoping to hear the response that I felt was due.

The truth was he had no response. While I thought he would have been so excited to hear this news, being that we literally spent hours talking about our future together, and the life we would live. We talked about all three children we would have in addition to the five that were already here. The truth was, there was no excitement. There was no joy. There were no congratulations. There was no, "Babe, I am so happy." There was nothing but silence on the other end of the line.

The light that had filled my days had started to grow dim. My significant other, my partner, and my love was literally blowing my candle out. I felt coldness creep its way in and enwrapped me in her snare. The joy that had been birthed within me has been stolen away.

Once he knew that we were expecting, I felt that life stole my joy. There was a shift in our relationship, a change in the climate. Our communications became scarce, and when we did converse our exchange was dull. The excitement dissipated. There I was, holding a piece of him within me, but he was seldom to be found.

I felt fear's slithery and slimy body squeeze itself into my mind. Thoughts of uncertainty around my relationship placed great stress on me as I now had to consider raising this child on my own. This was not the way I had envisioned my life going.

About two weeks after the pregnancy confirmation, I noticed that I was passing blood. Fear did not hold its grip tighter around my mind as thought distortions pursued me. Flashbacks to pregnancy bleeding came flooding back as I remember the look on Markel's face when I learned that he had been unfaithful to me and caused the loss of our child. The thought that this baby was dying circumvented my mind. I knew what was happening, but I wasn't sure what could have caused it this time.

Despite the condition where which the child was conceived, I still wanted this child. I went to see my doctor, who checked my body and found nothing abnormal. He was unsure as to why the bleeding had commenced. The only advice was for me to wait another three weeks to do a preliminary sonogram, where the fetus would be big enough to be seen at that time. That would give him a clearer picture of what could be going on.

I continued to keep my bae informed, even though his interest was not focused there. He would still come by to see me, but there was a notable shift in our relationship. I was obviously losing him.

There was a gap in my life, and even though I was dealing with a plethora of uncertain events, I was still expected to work and provide for my five children. There was no one to fill in the gaps for me. I had to be my own gap filler. This was such a load to carry all alone, but somehow, I did not faint or falter.

Three weeks had passed but the bleeding continued on. During those three weeks, the doctor was checking my HCG levels which were rising indicative of a persisting pregnancy. The time had come for me to see the baby, as it was now big enough to be seen on a sonogram.

There I laid on the exam table, with my clothes off and gown opened to the back. I stared at the ceiling, fearfully anticipating what they would see. Anticipation held my hand, and fear caressed my shoulders. Doubt whispered her sweet words into my ears and sadness embraced me in her arms. I was accompanied by many, but loneliness conquered all. I couldn't understand how I found myself in this predicament.

At this point, homeboy ghosted me again. I texted and called, wanting to keep him informed of what was happening but my attempts were null and void.

The cold slab of gel splattered on my wrinkled tummy. I shuddered. I closed my eyes as the exam was underway. Every so often, I opened my eyes and looked up at the white ceiling. My eyes would dart over to the screen as I kept trying to peek over to see if I noticed anything familiar. I was looking for a sack of some sort, which would reveal the presence of life but it was so dark, and the sonographer must have felt my peering eyes, as she turned the screen away from my line of view. At that point, I just laid back and closed my eyes.

Chapter 32: The Present

148

The entire classroom sat in silence as the words rolled off my lips. Not one soul moved, much less took a breath.

Chapter 33: The Present

The wait seemed like forever, but finally, my doctor made his debut and entered the room.

I tried to make my assessments of the outcome based on the facial expressions being made as he read the report. There was no success for me.

"Grace, Your baby is lodged between the end of your fallopian tube and the corner of the upper portion of your uterus."

There was a renewed sense of hope. The baby was indeed alive! I felt the slight release of fear's claws on my shoulders.

"OK," I replied, kind of shaking my head indicating my understanding, while still yet confused as to what that fully meant.

"This baby will not survive. We need to stop the pregnancy before your uterus ruptures."

Oh. Fear grappled my shoulders and sunk its claws deep into my skin. I let out a loud wail. My eyes peered at the doctor with anger and confusion. I couldn't understand.

"OK…so what do we need to do?" I asked.

The doctor suggested I take this injection drug which was a form of chemotherapy. It was designed to stop the growth of the child, and once the cells ceased to multiply, the body would pass the tissue on its own. With all of the debilitating side effects of taking this chemotherapy, there was a possibility that it wouldn't work. The drug was designed to terminate pregnancies in the early stages and was less effective as the pregnancy prolonged.

Taking the drug was one of the scariest things I had to do. I was forewarned that after taking the drug, I would be toxic. I had to wipe down the bathroom after each and every use, and I had to be sure that I kept all my bodily fluids to myself.

After taking the chemo, I had to take a bi-daily trip to the lab to have my blood drawn to assess my HCG levels, which needed to be going down at a certain rate which would have determined if the treatment was successful or not.

After one week of lab visits, I went back to see the doctor who sadly informed me, the treatment did not work the way he needed to see it work. I figured that he was just going to give me another dose of the chemo drug to halt the growth of the baby.

"No, you are too far along for anything that we could prescribe you to work. We will have to surgically remove the baby."

I sat still, trying to process the words that he just spoke to me. It sounded like a jumble and my brain needed extra time to decipher and digest what was said.

"OK…so how will the surgery work?" I finally blurted out after what seemed like a whole 45-minute class session.

"We will first go through your belly button to see if we can get it that way. If not, we will have to cut you open like they do for a cesarean section and remove the baby that way."

My heart began to sputter like a dying car. I literally held my chest as he continued to speak.

"There are many risks with this surgery…"

He continued to list all the possible outcomes. I looked, listened, and nodded my head without truly cosigning. It really made no sense to me. I was still in disbelief that I was going through this experience.

"…If all else fails and we are unable to stop the bleeding, we will have to perform a complete hysterectomy."

I fainted.

After regaining consciousness, and ensuring that I was OK, the doctor informed me that he was able to perform the surgery the following day. I sat there in shock at all the news I heard and simultaneously tried to figure out what I would do with my other babies.

My heart ached immensely, as I thought of what I was about to endure. Where was my knight in shining armor? The one who had promised to be there for me? Even though I knew he wouldn't answer, I called. Even though I knew he wouldn't respond, I texted. Even though I knew he couldn't hear me, I cried out to him. I needed him, but there I was alone.

I remember that morning. I walked into the hospital. I sat and waited with fear brewing in my heart. I went in and completed all the pre-surgical formalities. Then I waited for my doctor to arrive. I was surrounded by so many people, but I felt so alone.

Once he came in, I was prepped for surgery. I remembered him holding my hands and saying to me that everything was going to be alright. He promised to take care of me. I found the most comfort in those words because that's all I ever wanted. I just wanted someone to take care of me.

I was rolled into the operating room and the crisp air caused the hair on my forearms to rise to attention. There was an abrupt swap in seasons, summer to winter in the blink of an eye. I shivered. It was probably due to the cold, but I knew that fear had a part to play as well. I looked up at the white ceiling. I saw the faces of my little angels. I saw his face. I missed him, but he was leaving me now. The time had come to physically have him removed from within me, body, mind, soul, and spirit. It was time.

It went black.

Chapter 34: Present Day

"Grace, it's all over."

I woke up to the sound of the doctor's voice, but all I could see were shadows and light. Everything was a blur in front of me. After several blinks, the shadows became figures that I could recognize.

I was met with his warm smile and calming voice. I was so happy to be alive, which meant I didn't bleed to death.

"Grace, everything went well. We did have to cut you open but, we were able to remove the pregnancy from the upper portion of your uterus while controlling the bleeding."

"Are all my organs still inside of me?" I asked with a high-pitched childlike tone.

"Yes, everything is still there." replied the doctor in a warm soothing melodic voice.

He explained to me all the wound care procedures I needed to follow, and after a couple of hours of monitoring, they discharged me home.

The weeks to follow that incident were nothing short of painful. I literally replayed all the words spoken to me, all the moments we shared, all the hopes and dreams we painted on a canvas that we were decorating together.

I can't believe that I loved someone who only loved himself. As I recapped and reflected on the relationship, it became more evident that it was always about him. I was blinded by my pain. I wanted everything to be OK so badly that I failed to see all the warning signs. I don't understand why I had to endure the pain of this encounter. Why was I unable to see clearly?

As time went on, I couldn't let go. All the horrid events that took place in my life resurfaced after the latest trauma. The wound that I have had all the days of my life since being a child had not yet healed and there were no more band-aids available that I could use to cover it up. It was exposed.

Several times I had to reach out to my mom to hold me up. Talking to her provided me with a safe space to be myself. She allowed me to release the anger and pain that had built up inside that no band-aid could cover. She gave me permission to feel the pain I had stowed away. I cried the biggest, ugliest tears ever! I asked all the questions that she couldn't answer but I asked them anyways and she listened.

I realized that the position I found myself in was a cover-up for the pain I experienced after my divorce. This relationship was a ploy, another band-aid to suppress the pain. My problem was, I didn't want to face the music, but now I have no choice and for the first time I can hear it clearly!

Walking away from Markel was indeed painful. It cost me additional pain because I did not allow myself to grieve the first pain. The latter pain could have claimed my life! Acknowledgment of this now affords me a freedom that was long overdue.

Giving myself permission to grieve and deal with the pain opened the portal to experience true healing. Grieving is a necessary 'evil' to activate the fullness of gratitude you can experience. Allowing myself to feel the pain allows for healing transformation to take place and opens the door to all the beautiful experiences life does have to offer.

By allowing myself to grieve and feel the pain, I was able to cut myself free from the mental bondage that prevented me from flourishing in the way that I was destined to. I was able to take a moment to sit with myself and force myself to process who I was and what had become of me. I learned that I had lacked self-love all these years. I neglected myself. I abused myself by accepting whatever happened to me without speaking up and defending myself.

I abandoned little childlike Grace by not speaking up for her in the present. I needed to give the past, childlike Grace her voice back.

Stepping away from the shadows of my 'enemies' gave me the opportunity to look at myself straight away in the mirror. I had to stand and face the jury. The jury was me...Grace. I had to open the container of my heart and unpack all of my baggage. I had stored so much in there over the course of the years.

Some days I felt strong, strong enough to unpack the mess. On other days, I couldn't endure two minutes without succumbing to explosive anger and tears. Even right now I have no real direction for my life, except that I am moving forward. I am allowing myself to flow and for my spirit to align where it needs to be.

Even now as I walk forward in the darkness, I trust my intuition, that inner guide, that still small voice that whispers through the clangs and clatter. That still, small voice will lead me on the paths that were designed just for me. Paths that will enable me to experience success, love, hope, joy, and peace.

Walking on this path is one of the hardest things I've ever had to do in my life. The mere fact that I am now taking a stand for myself is significant progress. I now know that I matter. My past experiences had many treacherous moments, but all of them come with an object lesson. This whole process of heartache and pain helped me to learn more about the kind of person that I am and the kind of person I actually want to be. I now understand what I want and what I actually deserve. I now know that I have to find myself. I have to pick up the pieces and live. My story is not over!

I was not whole! I now realized that I needed something in my life. I needed to achieve a state of wholeness. Wholeness starts with me letting go. I needed to truly let go of all the pain in my life starting with the abandonment of my father, the abuses endured by family members, as well as the betrayal and losses I've experienced. The art of forgiveness was what I needed to implement in my life so that I could truly live out the wholeness I have always longed for.

Chapter 35: Present Day

"Everyone loves to devour a moist slice of pineapple turnover cake, or better yet, a slice of grandma's sweet potato pie at Thanksgiving dinner. These delicious delights bring joy to our hearts and a smile to our souls. Have you ever considered that in order to make these treats perfect, they must contain all the ingredients in their correct proportions? There needs to be the right amount of sugar to salt, as well as enough pineapples to cover that cake! What if one of the ingredients were missing? How does this parallel our wholeness?"

In order for wholeness to be achieved, we must incorporate all the segmented components that make a person whole. There are so many different factors that contribute to wholeness but first and foremost, it takes the recognition and identification of the areas in our lives that have been worn and stripped away by the wears and tears of life, experiences, and circumstances, which have caused the disruption in our wholeness in the first place. Once there is clarity, step by step, each ingredient can be restored to achieve the wholeness we desire. There are so many ingredients that contribute to our wholeness such as authenticity, vulnerability, presence, and openness, but today I would like to focus on the ingredient of forgiveness.

I've lived a life of immense pain as early as nine years old. I've experienced pain inflicted upon me knowingly and unknowingly. While I can recall several moments in my life where I have been hurt, there were four distinct events, which I remember clearly where I was robbed. I was robbed of my innocence. I was robbed of my childhood. I was robbed of my authenticity, and I was robbed of my fragile heart. These events drastically shifted my life in a profound way.

I was robbed of my innocence when my eyes were opened to things that I had no business knowing about or experiencing at such a young age. I was robbed of my childhood, being exposed to activities that caused me to delve into a business in which I had no business participating. I grew up really fast. I was robbed of my authenticity, as I spent many years of my life, living a facade, using every tactic I could summon to live the life that everyone expected me to live, especially those who were very close to me. I totally dismissed what I truly felt or thought but rather prioritized everyone else's wants and needs above my own.

Lastly, I was robbed of my fragile heart. My heart was already broken, and I was at one of the lowest and most vulnerable places in my life and I was tricked and taken advantage of by another. Simply put, I was used, and then 'ghosted'.

Can you imagine the buried anger that's been suppressed over the years? I mean literally, stowed away! I've learned to mask the pain and let my ego lead the way. Here I'm thinking that I have all this pain and trauma packed away, and suppressed, never to rear its ugly head again.

Boy, was I wrong?

This anger was buried, festering for years. Imagine yourself as a child, running and playing freely, soon to find yourself staring at a deep gash and a pool of blood. Instead of going inside to momma, and having her doctor it up, you just put a band-aid on it yourself and continue as you were. Ignoring the wound most definitely won't make it disappear, but rather, not addressing it causes it to become infected. With continued ignorance of the matter, that once 'minor' wound can become a full-blown infection, affecting the entire body. Oh how this all could have been avoided, but that's not my point today.

My stowed-away anger was angry. It longed to be released and being met with resistance was causing it to wreak havoc. The anger within me was raging, and as much as I tried to contain it, it was spilling through my pores.

It was causing increased emotional numbness, depression, lack of motivation, and subconscious anger toward the guilty parties.

How could I be whole in this state? How can anyone be whole in this state? The missing ingredient to achieve the wholeness I sought was forgiveness.

In order to release the anger, the steam, and the pain, I need to forgive those who have hurt me. I have to release them as they have taken up residence in my heart and are no longer welcome. Forgiveness does not mean that you forget what happened to you. Unless you suffer from memory loss, God forbid, you will always remember. When you forgive, you release the pain associated with the events. You address the person who has caused your pain, letting them know what they did to you and how it made you feel. You keep it real with them 100%, but at the end of it, you let them know that you forgive them and you let the pain and anger go.

Forgiveness is an ingredient of wholeness. Releasing the anger and pain puts your heart and mind at ease. It gives you rest and peace and calms your system as it no longer has to work overtime to store away painful feelings and emotions. Forgiveness is liberating. Forgiveness is freedom.

Forgiveness is life. Abundant life. Forgiveness is me.

Our daily goal should be striving toward wholeness and forgiveness which is a necessary ingredient. During one of my counseling sessions, my therapist asked me the following thought-provoking questions:

"What have I learned about forgiveness? What does it take? What does forgiveness look like?"

I thought about those questions intently. In the past, I always thought that the moment you said to yourself, "I forgive that person." Or even if you tell them to their face, that forgiveness was readily attained at that moment.

Experience would teach me that it wasn't so simple. I've learned that saying "I forgive you" isn't enough. True forgiveness takes time. Time is necessary to face the pain and the trauma, squared up, face to face, like two people in a boxing ring. Pain is trying to reign triumphant here, but you have to face pain in the face, tell him he's a pain in the behind, look him in the eye and tell him to get out because he's no longer welcome.

You have to look at that trauma for what it is. Understand what happened, call it out, holding nothing back. You have to identify how it made you feel and the damage that it caused you. You have to allow your voice of truth to proclaim all it needs to say. Unfiltered.

It is at that moment, when the last sentence is spoken, the moment when the last adjective you used to describe your pain is revealed, the moment when you physically feel the ache of the trauma somehow vanish off your shoulders, that you can authentically set yourself free with the words, "I forgive you."

"I'm so overjoyed to say that I have forgiven those who have drastically altered my life. While the alteration wasn't in God's perfect will, He allowed me to go through this for my growth and for me to fulfill His purpose through me while I sojourn this life. Wholeness is a choice away. Add that forgiveness flavor. It's bitter at first but I promise you it's sweet at the end."

The class stood up and offered Grace a thunderous round of applause. Grace's eyes darted toward the floor with her face flushed red.

"Grace, your presentation was excellent. You opened us all to your world. We were able to see your past, your present, and the direction for your future. You helped us to understand that we are all faced with adversity in some way, shape, and form. We saw the impact that hurt, betrayal, and defeat could have on the heart of a child and even an adult. We also see the birth of an individual who found her voice and realized her own self-worth. Grace, thank you so much for your vulnerability," said Professor De Jesus coupled with a heartfelt hug.

I walked back to my seat feeling triumphant. I sat back in my chair and closed my eyes. I literally saw my life flash in front of my eyes. I saw the old me, and then I saw the new; the rebirthed me; the stronger me; the resilient me; the present me, I now needed to be for my children and for the world. I sat there, eyes closed, watching myself.

Somehow, I was able to get the old Grace's attention. I tapped her on the shoulder. She looked at me startled. I had so much to tell her. So much I wanted to share, but I only had a short amount of time to get my message across.

"Can I help you?" she asked.

I responded to her just like this:

"Where is that little black girl that I used to know?
Round and stout with the kinkiest black afro
Where is that little black girl that I used to see?
Playing freely with her toys and her favorite Barbie
Where is that little black girl who used to laugh so loud?
Her laugh was so contagious, it would immediately ignite a crowd.
Where is that little black girl whose imagination was so free? She would write about anything…You just let her be
Where is that little black girl who always used to smile?
A grin so wide, ear to ear, something she could not hide
That little black girl was robbed by life's woes
Innocence snatched by ravenous folks
Her smile, her glee, her freedom slipped away.
Traded with sadness, sorrow, and overwhelming dismay that little black girl should be looking ahead for all the joys that life should bring."

"*Who am I?*" I shouted at myself.

Little black girl…little black girl

You've experienced what we call life

This road is not easy, it's filled with undue strife

So realize in your pity, that you have to rise above

Look to the stars, reach for the clouds whose end is way, way up above.

Yes, you've had setbacks, yes, life is hard, and yes, you live with the weight of your past, bearing the biggest, ugliest, nastiest scar.

Raise the bar!

In the midst of your weight and constant state of doom

Tap into your inner greatness and let all your thoughts of greatness consume…You.

Arise out of this state of despair

You have little ones following behind you, so please beware.

Their success has some stance on the choices you make, so don't hesitate to be great!

"Little black girl…find your smile

Little black girl…find your joy

Little black girl, you were destined to be the greatest you…Stand tall and believe."

With closed eyes, I stared into space with the biggest, widest smile plastered on my face as I pondered the words that I told myself.

Professor De Jesus tapped me on my shoulder, and I opened my eyes to his warm smile.

"Grace, are you OK?" he gently asked.

I looked up at him and smiled.

"I am on my way to freedom," I replied.

"Out of the old I have been birthed anew and I am OK."

I thanked him quickly, grabbed my books and bag, and dashed out of the door to pick up my babies.

Chapter 36: Next Steps

Healing is truly a choice.

Today is the day when you can start your healing by first embracing the art of forgiveness.